DEADLY DISEASES AND EPIDEMICS

MALARIA

Anthrax

Cholera

HIV/AIDS

Influenza

Lyme Disease

Malaria

Mononucleosis

Polio

Syphilis

Toxic Shock Syndrome

Tuberculosis

Typhoid Fever

DEADLY DISEASES AND EPIDEMICS

MALARIA

Bernard A. Marcus

CONSULTING EDITOR
I. Edward Alcamo
Distinguished Teaching Professor of Microbiology,
SUNY Farmingdale

FOREWORD BY
David Heymann
World Health Organization

CHELSEA HOUSE PUBLISHERS
A Haights Cross Communications Company
Philadelphia

In memory of Ed Alcamo: Friend and Colleague.

—Bernard Marcus

8-11-04

Dedication

We dedicate the books in the DEADLY DISEASES AND EPIDEMICS series to Ed Alcamo, whose wit, charm, intelligence, and commitment to biology education were second to none.

CHELSEA HOUSE PUBLISHERS

VP, NEW PRODUCT DEVELOPMENT Sally Cheney
DIRECTOR OF PRODUCTION Kim Shinners
CREATIVE MANAGER Takeshi Takahashi
MANUFACTURING MANAGER Diann Grasse

Staff for Malaria

ASSOCIATE EDITOR Beth Reger
PRODUCTION EDITOR Megan Emery
PHOTO EDITOR Sarah Bloom
SERIES DESIGNER Terry Mallon
COVER DESIGNER Keith Trego
LAYOUT 21st Century Publishing and Communications, Inc.

A Haights Cross Communications Company

http://www.chelseahouse.com

First Printing

1 3 5 7 9 8 6 4 2

Library of Congress Cataloging-in-Publication Data

Marcus, Bernard A.
  Malaria / Bernard Marcus.
     p. cm. — (Deadly diseases and epidemics)
Includes index.
Contents: On the wings of mosquitoes — A complex life cycle — The origin, evolution, and ecology of malaria — The discovery of plasmodium
— Diagnosis and treatment — Attempts at malarial control — Preventing malaria — Malaria now — The future of malaria.
  ISBN 0-7910-7466-8
  1. Malaria—Juvenile literature. 2. Malaria—History—Juvenile literature. [1. Malaria.] I. Title. II. Series.
  RA644.M2M213 2003
  616.9'362—dc22

                                                    2003019307

Table of Contents

Foreword

In the 1960s, infectious diseases—which had terrorized generations—
were tamed. Building on a century of discoveries, the leading killers
of Americans both young and old were being prevented with new
vaccines or cured with new medicines. The risk of death from
pneumonia, tuberculosis, meningitis, influenza, whooping cough,
and diphtheria declined dramatically. New vaccines lifted the fear
that summer would bring polio, and a global campaign was
approaching the global eradication of smallpox. New pesticides
like DDT cleared mosquitoes from homes and fields, thus reducing
the incidence of malaria which was present in the southern United
States and a leading killer of children worldwide. New technologies
produced safe drinking water and removed the risk of cholera and
other water-borne diseases. Science seemed unstoppable. Disease
seemed destined to almost disappear.

But the euphoria of the 1960s has evaporated.

Microbes fight back. Those causing diseases like TB and malaria
evolved resistance to cheap and effective drugs. The mosquito evolved
the ability to defuse pesticides. New diseases emerged, including
AIDS, Legionnaires, and Lyme disease. And diseases which have not
been seen in decades re-emerge, as the hantavirus did in the Navajo
Nation in 1993. Technology itself actually created new health risks.
The global transportation network, for example, meant that diseases
like West Nile virus could spread beyond isolated regions in distant
countries and quickly become global threats. Even modern public
health protections sometimes failed, as they did in Milwaukee,
Wisconsin in 1993 which resulted in 400,000 cases of the digestive
system illness cryptosporidiosis. And, more recently, the threat from
smallpox, a disease completely eradicated, has returned along with
other potential bioterrorism weapons such as anthrax.

The lesson is that the fight against infectious diseases will
never end.

In this constant struggle against disease, we as individuals have
a weapon that does not require vaccines or drugs, the warehouse
of knowledge. We learn from the history of science that "modern"
beliefs can be wrong. In this series of books, for example, you will

learn that diseases like syphilis were once thought to be caused by eating potatoes. The invention of the microscope set science on the right path. There are more positive lessons from history. For example, smallpox was eliminated by vaccinating everyone who had come in contact with an infected person. This "ring" approach to controlling smallpox is still the preferred method for confronting a smallpox outbreak should the disease be intentionally reintroduced.

At the same time, we are constantly adding new drugs, new vaccines, and new information to the warehouse. Recently, the entire human genome was decoded. So too was the genome of the parasite that causes malaria. Perhaps by looking at the microbe and the victim through the lens of genetics we will to be able to discover new ways of fighting malaria, still the leading killer of children in many countries.

Because of the knowledge gained about such diseases as AIDS, entire new classes of anti-retroviral drugs have been developed. But resistance to all these drugs has already been detected, so we know that AIDS drug development must continue.

Education, experimentation, and the discoveries which grow out of them are the best tools to protect health. Opening this book may put you on the path of discovery. I hope so, because new vaccines, new antibiotics, new technologies and, most importantly, new scientists are needed now more than ever if we are to remain on the winning side of this struggle with microbes.

David Heymann
Executive Director
Communicable Diseases Section
World Health Organization
Geneva, Switzerland

1

On the Wings of Mosquitoes

BATTLE ZONE

In the autumn of 1942, American Marines were dug into the sands on the Island of Guadalcanal in the South Pacific, about to face one of the bloodiest battles in World War II. The Japanese had occupied Guadalcanal and the surrounding islands since January of that year. In August, the Marines gained control of the island, but the Japanese did not retreat quietly. Fierce fighting continued through February 1943. However, in the autumn, while the Marines worried about the coming battle and the enemy they had to face, mosquitoes hummed about them incessantly and bit them mercilessly, especially after dark. The mosquitoes were at their worst just after dusk and just before dawn. Sleeping under those conditions was probably next to impossible. Perhaps the Marines did not worry about the mosquitoes as much as they did about the coming battle, but perhaps they should have. The mosquitoes were more than just a nuisance.

Thanks to the development of **antibiotics**, World War II was perhaps the first war in history where more men died from wounds suffered in battle than from infections. Previously, those who were not mortally wounded often developed infections that could not be cured, and in the crowded, stressful, dirty conditions of battle, contagious infections passed easily from one person to another, especially if they were malnourished. However, Guadalcanal and perhaps other jungle-covered South Pacific islands remained places where illness continued to take more lives than did fighting (Figure 1.1).

Diseases of Entomological Importance

World War II

United States Armed Forces, 1940-45

Disease	1940-1941	1942-1943	1942-1945
Diarrhea, Dysentery	20,976	199,505	523,331
Dengue Fever	656	23,192	84,093
Malaria	8,233	178,594	460,936
Filariasis	0	--	1,653
Sand fly fever	0	--	12,438
Scabies	--	21,286	--
Typhus	0	0	7,352

Data from Statistical Health Reports, Division of Medical Statistics, Office of the Surgeon General, Department of the Army

Figure 1.1 Many diseases hindered the United States Military during World War II, malaria being one of the most prevalent. As shown in this chart, diarrhea and dysentery hampered the troops most frequently during the first two years, with malaria not posing as great a problem. By 1942, however, there were nearly as many cases of malaria among servicemen as there were cases of diarrhea and dysentery.

Seventeen hundred American men died from wounds suffered during the Battle of Guadalcanal. Four to five thousand died of the disease spread by the mosquitoes: malaria. The

Japanese may have suffered even higher casualties, from both the fighting and the mosquitoes. When wounded American survivors were evacuated to Australia, many were placed in a particular hospital near a swamp, where mosquitoes spread the disease among them even more. Indeed, at one point, General Douglas MacArthur, Commander of U.S. forces in the Southwest Pacific during World War II, is said to have complained that at any time, one third of his troops had malaria and another third was recovering from it. In fact, it was not until commanders were made responsible for their troops' health that precautionary

MOSQUITO TAXONOMY

Taxonomy is the branch of biology that deals with the classification of plants and animals. It begins with a broad, all-inclusive category, the kingdom. Each category is divided into more specific subcategories that are based on particular characteristics of the organisms being classified. The following is the taxonomy of malaria mosquitoes.

KINGDOM: Animals

    PHYLUM: Arthropods (animals with paired, jointed legs and an external skeleton)

        CLASS: Insects (arthropods with three pairs of jointed legs)

            ORDER: Diptera (flies–insects with one pair of wings)

                FAMILY: Culicidae (the mosquitoes)

                    GENUS: *Anopheles*

measures were taken to avoid malarial infection. Troops were ordered to take quinine tablets daily to avoid becoming infected. Once the administering of quinine tablets became policy, malaria was brought under control, and the Americans could go about their task of winning the war in the Pacific.

MOSQUITO-BORNE DISEASE

Malaria is one of many diseases spread by mosquitoes, and mosquitoes are by no means the only **arthropods** (small animals with jointed legs, including the mosquitoes) that feed on human blood and spread disease.

The blood of any animal is a rich source of nourishment for any other organism that can take advantage of it. Small animals, such as mosquitoes and other blood-sucking arthropods, are well adapted to such a lifestyle because they are usually able to make contact with their victims without being detected, grab a quick meal, and disappear without being swatted (Figure 1.2). Other much larger animals, like the sea lamprey of the Great Lakes and Atlantic Ocean, readily feed on the blood of large fish like salmon or lake trout. Organisms that feed on the tissues of animals without killing them first are referred to as **parasites**. Those that do so without actually entering the bodies of their victims are referred to as **ectoparasites**. Ectoparasites survive by feeding on other animals, but they do not kill them in the process. Mosquitos are ectoparasites. Still there are other parasites—usually smaller organisms—that live inside their victims and, consequently, inside their nutrient supply. Such parasites do not have to go looking for a meal when they are hungry, nor do they worry much about being eaten by other animals. Such parasites are known as **endoparasites**. The organism that causes malaria (*Plasmodium*) is an endoparasite. A problem that theses parasites do face, however, is what to do should their host die. When that

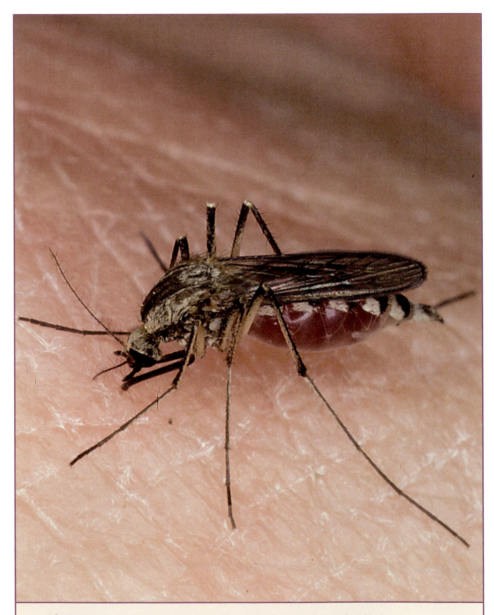

Figure 1.2 The mosquito, like the one pictured here, feeds on human blood and can transfer the malaria parasite from person to person. The malaria parasite, *Plasmodium*, does not harm the mosquito but can cause illness and even death in humans.

happens, the parasites within die as well, and it is not in a parasite's best interest to kill its host. Malaria and some other endoparasites get around this problem by hitching a ride from one victim to another via an ectoparasite. Such is the case with malaria, which hitches a ride from victim to victim within a mosquito.

Human malaria is always carried by a mosquito of the genus *Anopheles*. There are over 400 species of *Anopheles* mosquitoes, of which perhaps 60 can carry malaria. Mosquitoes of other genera may carry malaria among other animals, such as birds, but they appear to be incapable of spreading the disease among humans, even if they bite someone who is infected with the parasite. Moreover, malaria that affects other animals cannot be transferred to people. A specific relationship appears to exist among each species of malaria, each species of animal it affects, and the mosquito species that carries it. Only human malaria affects people, and only

SOME MOSQUITO-BORNE DISEASES

Dengue fever

Eastern equine encephalitis

Japanese encephalitis

LaCrosse encephalitis

Western equine encephalitis

West Nile virus

Yellow fever

Malaria

Elephantiasis

some specific species of *Anopheles* mosquitoes are capable of transmitting it.

Generally, an endoparasite such as the organism that causes malaria is referred to by biologists as simply a **parasite**. The mosquito that spreads it is called a **vector**. The victim within whom the parasite lives is called the **host**. Although malaria may have been brought under control among American servicemen in the South Pacific in World War II, it affects millions of people worldwide today. Each year there are approximately 100 million new cases of malaria and 1 million deaths associated with it.

Malaria is a complex disease that may occur in four different forms. The disease is caused by a protozoan of the genus *Plasmodium*, and it is spread by mosquitoes of the genus *Anopheles* (Chapter 2). For much of human history it has caused illness, suffering, and death, and it has had a major impact on history. Today, malaria remains a serious medical challenge in much of the world, particularly in Africa.

This book describes the *Plasmodium* life cycle in Chapter 2, the *Anopheles* life cycle as well as the origin and ecology of the disease in Chapter 3, and the impact of malaria on

SOME BLOOD-SUCKING ARTHROPODS AND THE DISEASES THEY SPREAD

Ticks: Lyme disease, Rocky Mountain spotted fever, typhus

Fleas: Bubonic plague

Tsetse flies: Sleeping sickness

Sandflies: Leishmaniasis (kala-azar)

Black flies: River blindness

Reduviid bugs: Chagas disease

history in Chapter 4. In Chapter 5, the book talks about the medical diagnosis and treatment of malaria, its control in Chapter 6, and prevention in Chapter 7. The book concludes with the current state of malaria in Chapter 8 and what the future may hold in Chapter 9.

2

A Complex Life Cycle

The term *malaria* originates from the Italian word *mal'aria*, meaning bad air. The Romans knew about malaria 2,000 years ago. They believed that malaria was caused by foul air that resulted from fermentation that seeped out of marshes and swamps. It is now known that malaria is spread by *Anopheles* mosquitoes. The disease is caused by a protozoan, a single-celled endoparasite of the genus *Plasmodium*.

THE PARASITE

There are more than 50 species of *Plasmodium*, only four of which cause human malaria: *Plasmodium falciparum*, *Plasmodium malariae*, *Plasmodium ovale*, and *Plasmodium vivax*. *Plasmodium vivax* is the most common. It usually causes a mild and very rarely fatal form of

---

PLASMODIUM TAXONOMY

KINGDOM: Protista

PHYLUM: Apicomplexa

CLASS: Sporozoasida

ORDER: Eucoccidiorida

FAMILY: Plasmodiidae

GENUS: *Plasmodium*

---

malaria. Similarly, *Plasmodium ovale* causes a mild infection. *Plasmodium malariae* causes a severe fever, but it is not usually life threatening. In contrast, *Plasmodium falciparum* causes severe infection that kills millions of people every year worldwide. *Plasmodium falciparum* is the organism that causes the form of malaria that is classically thought of whenever the disease is mentioned.

The *Plasmodium* life cycle (Figure 2.1) is described as an **alternation of generations**. This means an asexually reproducing generation, which reproduces by splitting in two, alternates with a generation that reproduces by forming sex cells that fuse with one another and produce individuals with new combinations of traits.

When an infected mosquito bites a person, the *Plasmodium* parasites enter the blood and head immediately for the liver. Within 30 minutes to one hour, all of the parasites have penetrated the liver; none remain in the circulating blood. Once inside the liver, the organisms multiply asexually, which means that each one divides into two identical copies of itself. They continue this reproduction in the liver cells for nine to 16 days, after which they emerge from the liver and invade red blood cells. The parasites mature in the red blood cells, where they feed on hemoglobin and continue to reproduce asexually. Eventually they burst out of the blood cells, rupturing them in the process.

After the first few reproductive cycles in the red blood cells, the maturation of all of the parasites becomes more or less coordinated, and the blood cells begin to rupture quite simultaneously. As the blood cells burst, the parasites and their waste products are released. The newly liberated parasites quickly infect new cells. This series of events repeats several times. Eventually, however, the asexual stage of the malaria cycle comes to an end, and the final generation of parasites emerges from the blood cells. Most of them reinvade the liver, where they may remain for a long time.

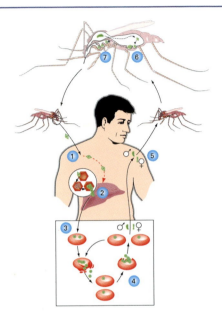

1. Mosquito infected with *Plasmodium* bites human.
   Plasmodium from mosquito salivary glands enter bloodstream

2. *Plasmodium* invades the liver and starts to reproduce

3. *Plasmodium* enters red blood cells

4. Further reproduction of the parasite causes red blood cells to burst.
   Other red blood cells become infected.
   Cycles of red blood cell infection and destruction coincide with fever
   and chills

5. Mosquito bites human and picks up *Plasmodium* reproductive cells

6. *Plasmodium* reproduces

7. *Plasmodium* migrates to mosquito salivary glands

Figure 2.1 *Plasmodium* has a complex life cycle, as depicted
in this diagram. First, the *Plasmodium* enters the human bloodstream while a mosquito is feeding on the blood. Second, the
Plasmodium parasite travels to the liver where it reproduces
several times and then leaves the liver for red blood cells. It
continues to replicate in red blood cells, causing them to burst,
thus releasing the parasite into the blood stream. The parasite
can then be picked up by another mosquito feeding on the
blood of the human carrier. *Plasmodium* reproduces again in the
gut of the mosquito and then travels to the mosquito's salivary
gland where it can be transferred back into the bloodstream of
a human the next time the mosquito feeds.

Some of these newly emerged parasites, however, become sexually reproducing cells. If an *Anopheles* mosquito bites a person when these cells are present in the blood and picks up any of them, the malarial life cycle continues into its sexually reproducing generation.

If a mosquito of a genus other than *Anopheles* bites someone with malaria, it simply digests any malarial cells that it swallows. However, *Plasmodium* can resist the digestive chemicals of the *Anopheles* mosquito digestive system, and when an *Anopheles* mosquito swallows the malarial reproductive cells that it has obtained from an infected victim's blood, each of the cells fuses with another in the mosquito's gut. The cells that result are described as **diploid**, because they have two identical sets of chromosomes: one from each of the cells that produced them. These new cells penetrate the wall of the mosquito's intestine. In the intestine, they undergo **meiosis**, a form of cell division that returns their chromosome number to one set per cell, known as **haploid**. These cells continue to divide, but they do not remain in the intestinal wall. Instead, after about ten days to two weeks, they migrate to the mosquito's salivary gland. When the mosquito bites a subsequent victim, it injects the parasites into the victim. The mosquito remains capable of infecting every person it bites until it dies. Infection with malaria parasites seems to make mosquitoes more active feeders.

Each of the four types of malaria has its own life cycle. *Plasmodium falciparum* has a faster reproductive rate and a shorter incubation period before symptoms of malaria show than do the other species. For example, it takes *Plasmodium malariae* up to 72 hours to complete a single generation inside a human host's red blood cells. *Plasmodium vivax* does it in 43 hours. *Plasmodium falciparum* takes as little as 36 hours to complete a generation in a human host's red blood cells. Additionally, *Plasmodium falciparum* cells may occupy as many as 60 percent of its host's red blood cells. Other malaria species usually occupy fewer than 2 percent.

AN INTRODUCTION TO PARASITOLOGY

Some parasites, such as *Plasmodium,* are incapable of surviving outside of a host organism. Thus, if this parasite kills its host, it will not survive unless a compatible transporting agent, such as a mosquito, picks it up. For this reason, a successful parasite is usually most at home in an organism that has a tolerance for that parasite. The parasite can complete its life cycle in such an organism without killing the organism or even making it sick. For example, the parasite that causes African sleeping sickness routinely lives in the large grazing animals of Africa. It is transported to humans only when a fly that has bitten an infected animal bites a human. The grazing animals in which the parasite is normally found are known as the **reservoir hosts** of the parasite. When the parasite gets into a human, it is still able to complete its life cycle. Because humans are not the normal home of the parasite, they are known as an **alternative host**. Nevertheless, the alternative host is often made ill and is sometimes killed by the parasite. Such is the case with sleeping sickness parasite, which can sometimes cause death to its human alternative host.

In the case of malaria, humans who are partially immune to the disease appear to be the reservoir host. Nonimmune humans act like the alternative hosts. The mosquito plays two roles. It is the **vector**, the means of transport from host to host. However, the parasite also needs the mosquito to complete its life cycle. That makes the mosquito a necessary part of the host-parasite cycle that is called the **intermediate host**.

Because the malaria life cycle involves more than one host, it is more complex than many other parasites. Whenever a parasite shows an alternation of generations in separate hosts, it reproduces sexually in only one of them. That host is known as the **definitive host**. In the case of malaria, the definitive host is the mosquito. To summarize then, humans play the role of the reservoir host. Mosquitoes play the role of vector, alternative host, and definitive host.

PARASITOLOGY

A parasite is defined as an organism that can live on or in another organism (a host) at the host's expense. Thus, a parasite in some way harms its host, either by competing with the host for nutrients or by slowly eating its host. A parasite that lives on the host, such as a flea or a skin bacterium, is called an ectoparasite. One that lives within the host, for example the *Plasmodium falciparum* parasite, is called an endoparasite. If the parasite cannot complete its life cycle outside of a host, it is called an obligate parasite.

An organism that normally lives on its own but can become parasitic if the opportunity arises is known as a facultative parasite. For example, the bacterium *Clostridium tetani*, the organism that causes tetanus, is a facultative parasite. Usually, this organism lives freely in the soil. But when it finds itself in dead tissue surrounding a deep puncture wound, as when someone steps on a rusty nail, it adjusts to living as a parasite.

Living on or in one's food source is ideal. Consequently, parasitism is a very successful life style. Some organisms, such as nematodes, are extremely common endoparasites. They carry on their entire lives within their hosts, rather than being a parasite only when the opportunity presents itself, as is the case with *Clostritium tetani*. Such an organism is called a permanent parasite. Another type of parasite is one that visits only for a meal, such as a mosquito or horsefly. This is a temporary parasite.

Permanent endoparasites often make their hosts ill. It is not in their best interests to kill their host. Doing so may kill the parasite as well. Some parasites avoid this problem by abandoning their host, possibly causing its death in the process. Some flatworms that parasitize snails are an example of such an endoparasite-host relationship. Other parasites cannot abandon their host; however, they do shed their eggs before they die, thus, ensuring the survival of their offspring and future generations of their species.

As mentioned earlier, there are 50 or more species of *Plasmodium*, and only four of those species cause human malaria. Other species cause malaria in other animals, from reptiles to apes. Similarly, of the 400 or more species of *Anopheles* mosquitoes, perhaps 60 are capable of serving as alternative hosts and vectors for human malaria. There are no rules specifying that they can bite only humans, of course, and it would seem logical that human malaria could be spread to other animals. But human malaria usually does not infect other animals, other than *Plasmodium malariae*, which may affect apes or monkeys. The *Plasmodia* of human malaria are human parasites only.

It would seem equally logical that the *Plasmodia* that cause malaria in other organisms would infect humans rather regularly as well. However, whenever those parasites are passed to humans, they are immediately destroyed by the human immune system. Unlike the parasites that cause malaria in humans, they have not evolved the ability to avoid our immune system.

Finally, *Anopheles* mosquitoes do not spread the malaria parasites of other animals. They are spread by other genera of mosquitoes. Exactly how malaria became a human disease and how the *Anopheles* mosquito became the vector is unknown. The thinking on the subject that now exists is discussed in the next chapter.

The incubation period for *falciparum* malaria in human blood before symptoms begin to show is between 10 and 14 days, during which time the parasites undergo several reproductive cycles and their numbers grow. Once the population of parasites has become large enough, the rupture of the blood cells and the release of parasites (Figure 2.2) causes the victim to feel chills, one of the most common symptoms. The waste products released into the blood stream trigger a reaction that several hours later culminates in the fever spikes associated with malaria.

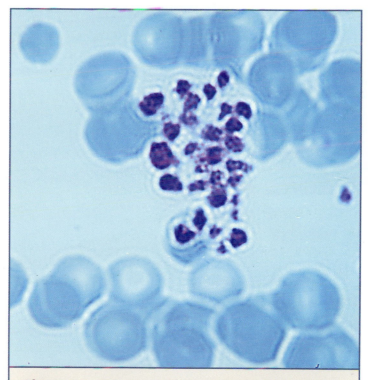

Figure 2.2 This photomicrograph shows *Plasmodium falciparum* gametocytes (reproductive cells) being released from a ruptured red blood cell. The gametocytes can now be picked up by another mosquito feeding on the host's blood.

Additionally, the removal of waste products from the blood by the kidneys causes a darkening of the urine, often referred to as blackwater urine. Headache, nausea, vomiting, joint pain, and body aches may accompany the fever. In the case of *Plasmodium falciparum*, symptoms can include brain infection, nervous dysfunction and confusion, progressive lethargy, seizures, and coma. Additionally, the victim can experience pulmonary edema (fluid in the lungs), dry cough, and anemia. Waste products can also lodge in the liver and spleen, where they cause damage. Eventually, however, the kidneys may fail. In up to 25 percent of cases, death will result.

Figure 2.3 One of the common symptoms of malaria is lethargy and extreme fatigue. The woman pictured above is suffering from malaria in a clinic in Nigeria, Africa.

In the non*falciparum* malarias, the outlook is less dire. Death is rarely an outcome. Instead, the symptoms occur every two to three days and last from four to six hours each, and occur less frequently over time. Symtoms include confusion, exhaustion, and extreme sweating (Figure 2.3). Recovery usually occurs in one to four weeks. When someone recovers from *falciparum* malaria, they usually do not have any lingering symptoms. However, the other types of malaria can become chronic. After recovery, the parasites can hide in the tissues and erupt years, even decades, later. Reoccurrences can occur for as long as 50 years. Additionally, the disease can remain infective. There was fear that survivors from the South Pacific in World War II would bring chronic malaria back to the United States and possibly start outbreaks here. There are, after all, several species of *Anopheles* mosquitoes that are common in North America, and at least some of them are compatible with *Plasmodium.*

THE VICTIMS

Mosquitoes are more likely to bite men than women, because mosquitoes are attracted to heat, and men give off more body heat than women do. This does not mean that mosquitoes will not bite women, however, including ones who are pregnant, and they will bite children as well, often preferentially because children give off more heat than adults. Malaria can be very serious in children and pregnant women, and *falciprum* malaria may develop into cerebral malaria in children. When this happens, red blood cells containing the parasite become isolated in the child's brain to the point that blood vessels may be blocked. Death can result. Death can also result to a fetus of a pregnant woman or to the pregnant woman herself. In Africa, where malaria is most common, such deaths are common.

3

The Origin, Evolution, and Ecology of Malaria

ORIGIN AND EVOLUTION

In the movie *Jurassic Park*, scientists were able to create dinosaurs by extracting DNA from mosquitoes that had bitten dinosaurs. The mosquitoes had become trapped in tree resin while resting after their meal. When the resin hardened to amber, the mosquitoes became fossilized. The blood meal and DNA they had eaten remained intact. Sixty-five million years later, the scientists extracted the DNA from the fossilized mosquito and inserted it into an egg of a frog. A dinosaur hatched as a result.

Although the film's events might today sound far fetched, cloning technology may one day advance to the point where DNA extracted from a fossilized mosquito will be used to generate an extinct organism, but the organism will not be a dinosaur. The dinosaurs became extinct over 65 million years ago. Mosquitoes have been around for less than half that time. How mosquitoes originated is not really known, but they have been biting ever since.

Likewise, the origin of *Plasmodium* is also unknown, although scientists believe that it originated in Africa around 30 million years ago. It probably was well established in people in Africa as many as 100 thousand years ago. Even today, Africans are more resistant to malaria than Europeans, which supports the idea of malaria's African origin.

Some scientists believe that *Plasmodium* was originally a parasite of other animals, probably birds. One hypothesis states that malaria became a human parasite after humans domesticated birds. In fact, *Plasmodium falciparum* appears to be more closely related to bird malarias than monkey malarias. The other three species of human malarias are more closely related to monkey malarias, and it is remotely possible that some transmission of them between humans and monkeys can occur. It is hypothesized that *falciparum* malaria was accidentally transferred to people, perhaps by the blood of an infected bird contaminating an open sore on the hand of a person butchering it. However the transfer occurred, malaria became successful as a human parasite, particularly as people became more and more abundant and replaced other animals as they became extinct.

Illnesses of animals that are transferred to people are known as **zoonoses** (singular **zoonosis**). Many common illnesses of humans, such as influenza, probably originated as zoonoses other than *Plasmodium falciparum*. Because *Plasmodium* is so specific to humans, it is doubtful that all malarias originated as zoonoses. More likely, they became parasites of our anthropoid (ape-like) ancestors, evolving with them to become parasites of humans.

ECOLOGY OF MALARIA I:
The Life Cycle of the Vector

The ecology of malaria depends entirely on the life cycle of the *Anopheles* mosquito (Figure 3.1). The success of *Plasmodium* in completing its life cycle is intimately tied to the success of the *Anopheles* mosquito in completing its life cycle, which can be difficult. The mosquito's life is constantly in danger, and its lifespan is very short.

A mosquito's life is critically dependent on water, where the female lays her eggs. She can lay eggs in bodies as small as birdbaths, drainage ditches, and discarded paper cups. Humans have contributed to the creation of breeding areas which will be discussed later in the chapter. In colder regions, the eggs may remain dormant over the winter. The eggs hatch when the water warms in the spring. After larvae hatch from the eggs (Figure 3.2), they live suspended from the surface of the water, breathe through an air tube, and eat organic matter,

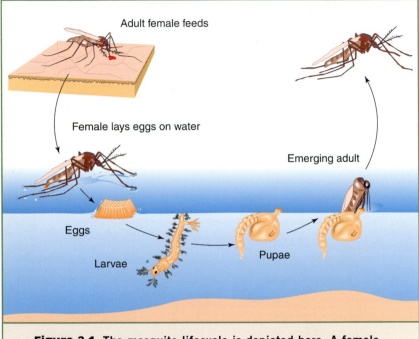

Adult female feeds

Female lays eggs on water

Emerging adult

Eggs

Larvae

Pupae

Figure 3.1 The mosquito lifecycle is depicted here. A female mosquito lays her eggs on the surface of a body of water. When the eggs hatch, they are called larvae. As the larvae grow, they turn in to pupae, which swim freely in the water. Finally, the pupae turn into adult mosquitoes, which leave the water and hunt for food.

which they filter through their mouthparts. Known as "wrigglers" because of their swimming motion, the larvae swim toward shelter if anything disturbs them. Many larvae are eaten by predacious insects and small fish. Those that survive grow. Each larva sheds its skin four times, a process known as molting. Then, it changes into a pupa. The pupa, known as a tumbler, swims freely, but remains vulnerable to predators. Once it becomes an adult, it leaves the water and flies to a nearby tree to rest and gather its energy. In the air the mosquito is vulnerable to bats, swallows, dragonflies, and any other flying predator. Mosquitoes that escape flying predators run the risk of flying into a spider's web. Those that make it to a tree are

Figure 3.2 After a mosquito egg hatches, the offspring is known as a larva, shown here. The larva will molt four times before becoming a pupa.

often eaten by ants. Very few mosquitoes, perhaps one in ten or less, live long enough to bite anybody. Of those that do, only the female bites. The male feeds on plant nectar. Female mosquitoes mate only once in their lives. Mating usually occurs shortly after they emerge as adults (Figure 3.3).

FINDING THEIR MEALS

One of life's more annoying petty experiences is to lie in bed at night with mosquitoes humming in your ears. You cannot see them to swat them, but they seem to know exactly where you are. Furthermore, why are they attracted to your ears?

Mosquitoes do not see well during the daytime. They can see movement and are attracted to it. They can also see an object that contrasts with its background. However, they are especially attracted to the carbon dioxide (CO_2) we exhale, to the warmth that radiates from our bodies, and to the

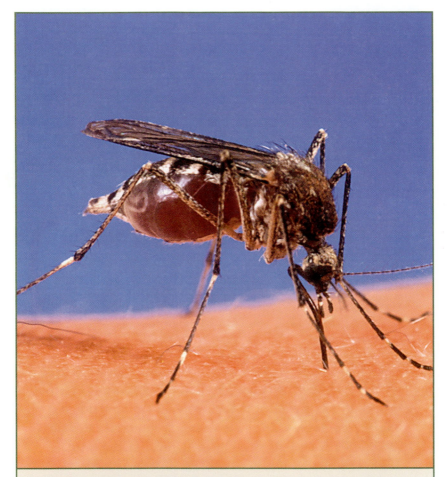

Figure 3.3 Only the female mosquito feeds on blood. The male mosquito prefers plant nectar. The adult mosquito pictured here is currently feeding on human blood. Notice that her body is engorged from her meal.

moisture that we emit through perspiration and respiration. A mosquito can sense the CO_2 in our breath from as far as 35 meters (about 100 feet) away. In addition, our blood carries heat from deep within our bodies, heat that is radiated by our skin to keep us from overheating. Mosquitoes can "see" this heat as infrared light through sensors on their antennae, and they are attracted to it. Because our ears are highly vascularized, which means that they are richly supplied with blood vessels, they radiate a lot of heat. Consequently, in a dark room, a person's ears look like a buffet table to a mosquito. Ironically, mosquitoes are blind to the ultraviolet "bug" lights that many people suspend in their yards. The lights are effective against some flying insects such as moths, which are attracted to ultraviolet lights, but not mosquitoes. Finally, there are chemicals in perspiration that mosquitoes can smell. People who perspire heavily attract more mosquitoes than do people who do not sweat readily, because both the moisture they give off and the chemicals in sweat attract mosquitoes.

Only the female mosquito bites. She requires a meal of blood to produce her eggs. The female mosquito drinks two or more times her weight in blood. After feeding, she flies to a vertical surface, such as a wall, and digests her meal. At this time, she may be vulnerable to hunting spiders or other insects that may also be nearby.

One problem a mosquito must solve is to prevent her victim's blood from coagulating as she feeds. She accomplishes this by injecting an anticoagulant into the tissue surrounding the bite. The welt and itch that accompanies a mosquito bite is an allergic reaction to the anticoagulant.

ECOLOGY OF MALARIA II:
Its Distribution and Transmission

Mosquitoes in general and *Anopheles* mosquitoes in particular have adapted to virtually every environment on Earth where fresh water is available. Consequently, malaria has become a cosmopolitan disease, meaning that it occurs worldwide. However, it is most problematic in Africa, especially south of the Sahara Desert, where it kills one child every 30 seconds on average. The mosquito present there, *Anopheles gambiae*, is well adapted to coexisting with people. It prefers human blood, and it feeds by day, when people are outside. Moreover, it can breed in as little water as the amount that accumulates in a hoof print after a rain; virtually all other species of mosquitoes need larger volumes. *Anopheles gambiae* typically bites every other day. It takes only 12 days for *Plasmodium falciparum* to complete the stage of its life cycle that occurs in mosquitoes. Roughly 30 percent of all mosquitoes that have bitten a person infected with malaria live long enough to bite a second victim and thus spread the disease. That may not seem like much, but mosquitoes multiply by the thousands. The commonality of malaria testifies to the survival success of those mosquitoes.

ECOLOGY OF MALARIA III:
Persistence and Tolerance of the Disease

Immunity to any disease often results from exposure to that disease. This applies to malaria but not perfectly. Human malarias appear to have evolved the ability to avoid the human immune system, and humans cannot develop a complete immunity to malaria as we can with, for example, smallpox. It is possible, however, to develop a partial immunity to malaria. In this case, a survivor would remain infected with the parasites, but he/she would not show symptoms of the disease.

The ability to generate resistance to a disease is initially genetic—that is, people must have the genes that will allow them to develop a resistance. Those people who do not are more likely to die. As a result, those who are resistant are more likely to survive and pass on their resistance to their offspring. Consequently, a population that is constantly exposed to malaria is most likely to be resistant. The disadvantage of that is that resistant people can serve as reservoirs for the parasite. For example, malaria is now common in Sri Lanka. Itinerant construction workers, subsistence farmers, and others without permanent housing are sufficiently resistant to the disease to survive and reproduce while infected with it.

They continue to be the reservoir in that country. It is ironic that a population's resistance to malaria requires ongoing infection. If malaria is eliminated from a population and then reintroduced after a couple of generations, everybody is vulnerable. An epidemic may result. Equally ironic is that when resistant people travel to areas where malaria is not present but compatible mosquitoes exist, they can take the disease with them and introduce it. This too can result in an epidemic.

Perhaps most ironic is the fact that there is a population of people that is truly immune to malaria, but they pay a heavy price for it. These are the people who have or carry a genetic condition known as sickle cell disease, sometimes called sickle cell anemia. This is an inherited disorder where the hemoglobin in the blood is shaped differently from normal hemoglobin (Figure 3.4). Someone who inherits this condition from both parents has so much abnormal hemoglobin that his red blood cells are distorted. Sickle cell hemoglobin does not carry oxygen well. The individual with the disease may suffer any number of symptoms, including pain, fever, and damage to organs. Without medical treatment, victims of this disease die young, often in childhood. However, someone who inherits the trait from only one parent has largely normal hemoglobin and is spared the worst consequences. He can live a relatively normal life, although he cannot live at very high altitudes. He is immune, however, to malaria because the *Plasmodium* parasite cannot survive in the modified red blood cell. Consequently, sickle cell disease provides persistent survival value to people who have it. It is a genetic protection against malaria, but because it can cause death in some circumstances, it is an imperfect solution.

SPREAD AND PERSISTENCE OF THE DISEASE

Even though malaria is considered to be a tropical disease, it has occurred in temperate and even semi-polar areas where

Anopheles mosquitoes exist. It is possible that an infected mosquito can be transported to an area where malaria is nonexistent and begin an epidemic. Malaria may have been transported from Africa to Brazil this way. The so-called tiger mosquito of the South Pacific, the vector for dengue fever, has recently been "shipped" to the Western Hemisphere. More commonly, however, an infected person travels into an area where there is no malaria, an *Anopheles* mosquito bites him, and the epidemic begins. Malaria has been transported all over the world.

Human activities have often ensured malaria's survival.

SICKLE CELL DISEASE

Sickle cell disease probably originated in Africa. This may explain why in the United States, it is most abundant among African Americans, affecting perhaps one in 400. However, sickle cell disease also occurs in the Middle East and around the Mediterranean Sea. It may have been brought there by African slaves. Any of those slaves or their descendents who later married into the native populations could have started spreading the gene among them. With the protection it offered against malaria, it would have easily survived any place where malaria was present.

Sickle cell disease is an inherited blood disorder that affects hemoglobin, the oxygen-carrying component of blood. Hemoglobin is made from protein, which is made of smaller components called amino acids. There are four protein chains in a hemoglobin molecule. In one of the chains, an amino acid is missing, substituted with another amino acid. The result is a hemoglobin molecule that is misshapen. The blood cell carrying that hemoglobin ends up misshapen as well.

Sickle cell disease causes a number of pathological problems. Sickle cell hemoglobin does not carry oxygen as well as normal

Construction areas, for example, have provided abundant breeding grounds. Mosquitoes now breed in places such as caves, troughs, birdbaths, drainage ditches, leech ponds, and poorly tended swimming pools. Discarded tires and other kinds of litter that can hold water have provided additional breeding grounds. Items as common as pottery vessels can also serve as a breeding ground. The construction of ponds and reservoirs, even backyard garden ponds, provide even more breeding grounds.

Anopheles mosquitoes typically breed in permanent bodies of water, although *Anopheles gambiae* may be

hemoglobin. In addition, it can cause heart enlargement, enlargement of the extremities, disturbed blood flow and blockage of small blood vessels, leg ulcers, susceptibility to infection, and early death.

The heredity of sickle cell disease follows the laws of simple dominance. To have the disease, one must inherit two recessive genes, one from each parent. Such an individual is said to be homozygous for the trait. Someone who inherits the gene from only one parent is described a being heterozygous. If two heterozygous individuals have a child together, there is a one in four chance that the child will be homozygous (i.e., will have the disease).

Treating sickle cell anemia is difficult. Currently, there are no genetic therapies. Antibiotics help prevent infection and, therefore, save many lives.

A screening test for carriers is available. Relatives of sickle cell victims who suspect they may have the disease can have the test. If a couple finds that they are both carriers, they can then decide whether or not to take their chances on having children of their own or adopting.

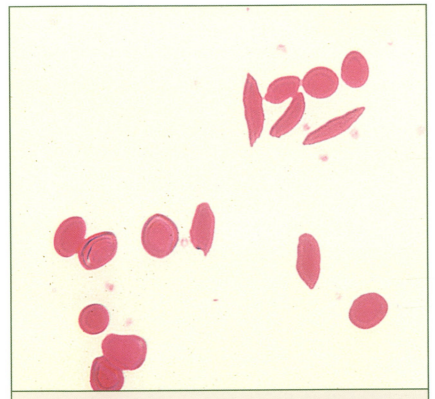

Figure 3.4 Sickle cell anemia is a disease that causes blood cells to become misshapen, often looking like "sickles," as can be seen in this micrograph. Sickle cells cannot carry oxygen as efficiently as normal blood cells. The disease also causes poor blood flow throughout the body and can result in death. Interestingly, people who have sickle cell anemia are resistant to malaria.

the conspicuous exception to this rule. Construction of permanent water bodies contributed to the population growth of these mosquitoes and their subsequent spread of malaria when the disease arrived in regions they inhabited. Thus, malaria may have made its way as far north as upstate New York, where it found a compatible mosquito and caused havoc during the construction of the Erie Canal. One bit of good fortune, however, was that *Plasmodium falciparum,* the most deadly form of malaria, was unable to survive the winters there. Even when an infected mosquito could survive the winter weather, *Plasmodium falciparum* was unable to become dormant. It usually died before the mosquito could start biting again in the spring. Still, malaria in its different forms managed to make its way around the world, and its impact on history was major.

4

The Discovery of *Plasmodium*

Scientists believe that malaria originated in Africa around 30 million years ago. Human malaria perhaps evolved into its current state along with our anthropoid and early human ancestors, although nobody really knows when. There is no record of its presence in Europe until the first century A.D., when it was first recorded in Rome. Most likely, malaria was brought to Rome by Roman troops returning from Africa or by the African slaves they brought with them. An *Anopheles* mosquito that was capable of spreading the disease inhabited the swamps around Rome.

Another hypothesis has it that malaria existed on the Italian peninsula for centuries before that. Its presence may have kept invaders from defeating Rome. For example, Hannibal's army from Carthage nearly succeeded in attacking the city of Rome in 218–201 B.C. However, he was stopped north of Rome, and some historians maintain that it was malaria that, at least in part, stopped him. Whichever hypothesis, if either, is correct, malaria did periodically cause the deaths of non-Italians, including invading armies. The native Italians, in contrast, who were constantly exposed to and probably continually infected with malaria, were able to maintain some resistance to the disease. Moreover, after the Roman Empire fell, the Italian peninsula continued to be protected by the endemic malaria. Although Rome may have been defeated, invaders never occupied the Italian peninsula. It was not until the twentieth century when Benito Mussolini, the ruler of Italy from 1922 to 1943, had the swamps around Rome drained that malaria was finally brought under control.

Although malaria may have protected Rome, it may also have contributed to its downfall. People infected with malaria are often lethargic. Lethargy is said to have characterized Rome later in the history of the empire. By the fourth century A.D., Roman legions were made up mostly of Germanic tribes, not Roman Italians. Ironically, Rome is said to have lost more than 40,000 of those legionnaires in Scotland to malaria during its campaign in the British Isles. When Rome did finally fall to the barbarians, the conquerors failed to occupy the Italian peninsula.

After the fall of Rome, European armies remained at home, for the most part. The Crusades were the conspicuous exception. Beginning with the voyages of Columbus, however, Europeans once again started claiming territory throughout the rest of the world. They established colonies throughout the Americas and much of Asia fairly easily, but not in Africa. Indeed, the colonization of Africa may have been delayed for 300 years by the endemic diseases of the continent, including malaria and yellow fever. In fact, some of Africa never came under European dominance because of malaria.

Malaria even interfered with European colonization in parts of Southeast Asia. For example, malaria was well established in New Guinea, especially in the lowland areas. It inhibited European settlement there. In contrast, Indonesians, who had been exposed to malaria for a long time and thus had immunity to the disease, had no trouble moving into New Guinea. The Europeans also had problems elsewhere in Asia. For example, the British lost many soldiers in India to malaria.

It is generally believed that malaria did not exist in the Western Hemisphere before Columbus discovered the Americas. It is also believed that malaria was brought to the United States by the Spaniards and by the European slave trade. Whether or not these theories are correct, it is likely that maritime traders brought malaria to the Americas from Europe; it was probably African slaves who brought malaria to North America, along with other African diseases. Once here, however, American *Anopheles* mosquitoes bit infected Africans, and the disease began to spread around and throughout the new world. Indeed, in the 1870s, malaria and yellow fever contributed to the failure of an attempt by the French to build a canal across Panama. Additionally, malaria delayed the exploration and colonization of much of what is now Brazil.

The spread of malaria throughout the United States and elsewhere in North America was assisted by a number of ironic twists. First, the organizers in Europe who were responsible for the decisions that brought malaria to the United States never left Europe. They never had to suffer the consequences of their decisions.

Second, the conversion of North America to a new Europe contributed to the spread of malaria in the United

MALARIA AS A CURE

One oddity in medicine is the use of one disease to treat another. In 1887, Julius Wagner-Jauregg, an Austrian psychiatrist, suggested that malaria could be used to treat syphilis. Theoretically, the high temperatures caused by malaria fevers would kill the syphilis bacteria. The idea never caught on because of the dangers inherent in malaria infection. However, by 1917, quinine was available for treatment of malaria. Wagner-Jauregg did use malaria to treat syphilis successfully in Austria after World War I. Whether the syphilis was cured because of the elevated temperature or some other reason, nobody knows. Today, however, as long as syphilis bacteria remain susceptible to antibiotics, it is unlikely that malaria will be used to cure it.

States. As North America was developed, agriculture became very important. Some of it, however, involved constructing irrigation ditches, water catchments, and even small ponds. Such structures caused standing water that provided ideal breeding conditions for *Anopheles* mosquitoes.

Agriculture was not the only change in North America that exposed immigrants to malaria. Other construction projects did as well. For example, the first important inland waterway constructed in North America was the Erie Canal. Built between 1817 and 1825, it connected the Hudson River in New York City to Lake Erie at Buffalo. The canal allowed commerce from New York City and the rest of the East Coast to upstate New York and midwestern cities that were on Lake Erie. West of Syracuse, the land through which the canal was slated to be built was very swampy. Currently, that region is the Montezuma National Wildlife Refuge, named most likely for the Aztec chief. At that time, the land was a mess of standing water and a mosquito hatchery. *Anopheles* mosquitoes are common in upstate New York. The introduction of malaria to the region, probably by an infected canal worker, was all it took to start a small epidemic. Many workers became ill and died with malaria during the construction of the canal. The illness may have delayed the completion of the project.

Upstate New York was not the only place in the United States affected by malaria. It was fairly common in the South, particularly in New Orleans, before World War II. Immigrant Irish laborers who worked in the swamps around New Orleans in the nineteenth century were especially victimized by the disease. Even the North, as evidenced by the experiences building the Erie Canal, was not spared. Elsewhere, Irish laborers working on public works projects in Boston during the nineteenth century also consistently encountered malaria.

For most of history, infections caused the largest number of deaths. Even during wars, more soldiers died from infected wounds than they did from the injuries themselves. World War II was the first war in which that was not the case, largely because of antibiotics. Most of the infections spread during war were bacterial, against which antibiotics worked. Malaria, however, was a conspicuous exception. It is caused by a protozoan, and the standard antibiotics had no effect on it. Moreover, in the South Pacific and East Asia, malaria continued to kill more Allied soldiers than battle did. Bringing malaria under control was crucial to the Allied victory in the South Pacific, and it continued to play an important role in world politics following the war.

The end of World War II brought about sweeping changes in the balance of world political power, which saw the planet divided essentially into two hostile camps. One, the Western Alliance, was dominated by the United States with the principal support of the nations of Western Europe. The other was dominated by Russia and the countries it absorbed as a result of World War II. Both camps tried to win influence with the rest of the world. Part of the strategy of the Western Alliance was to raise the living standards of the countries they were courting, and one part of their strategy was to provide medical aid. In the case of malaria, it was believed that the best strategy was prevention by controlling the vector. By that time, **DDT** (dichloro-diphenyl-trichloroethane, discussed further in Chapter 5), a potent insecticide, was available. DDT appeared to be effective against mosquitoes. By 1958, because of the use of DDT, victory against malaria was declared. In fact, medical schools stopped teaching about the disease. Subsequently, research on the disease was stopped, which turned out to be a big mistake. Malaria had receded, but it had not disappeared.

THE DISCOVERY OF *PLASMODIUM*

Among the reasons why malaria had such an impact on history was that people had no idea what caused the disease, nor how it was spread. As widespread as malaria is today, it is easy to overlook how much progress has been made against it during the past 150 years. It took almost 2,000 years for the cause of malaria to be discovered. In 1880, the French Army surgeon Charles Louis Alphonse Laveran (1845–1922) discovered the *Plasmodium* protozoan (Figure 4.1). Laveran, who also described the protozoan that causes sleeping sickness, was convinced that mosquitoes were responsible for spreading malaria. He was awarded the Nobel Prize in medicine in 1907.

Sir Patrick Manson (1844–1922), a Scottish physician, confirmed in 1900 that mosquitoes spread malaria. He accomplished this by allowing infected mosquitoes to bite volunteers. Manson had earlier discovered the worm that causes elephantiasis, a disease that causes swelling of the limbs, inside mosquitoes. This discovery may have given him the idea about malaria.

The third link in the chain of discovery of malaria was Sir Donald Ross (1857–1932), another British physician. Ross discovered the malaria parasite in the gut of a mosquito. Indeed, it was Ross's discovery that gave Manson the idea to have infected mosquitoes bite volunteers. It was Ross who was credited with confirming that *Anopheles* was the villain in human malaria. He had initially discovered the role of mosquitoes in spreading bird malaria. The real credit for the discovery may, however, be due to his Indian field assistant, Muhammed Bux.

BRINGING MALARIA UNDER CONTROL

Once the cause and transmission of malaria had become understood, steps could be taken to interrupt the cycle of the disease and reduce its impact. Swamps could be drained, windows could be screened, and care could be taken to remove standing water from structures on the ground. Even specific

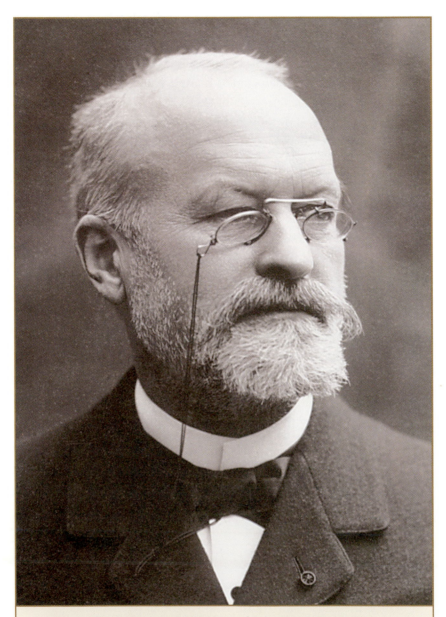

Figure 4.1 Charles Louis Alphonse Laveran, shown above, discovered *Plasmodium*, which causes malaria. He was awarded the Nobel Prize in Medicine in 1907 for his work on this parasite as well as his work on the role played by other disease-causing protozoa.

poisons could be used. Indeed, using these measures eventually brought malaria under control and almost totally eliminated it. Unfortunately, almost was not enough, and malaria has rebounded, as will be described in later chapters.

It is, of course, impossible to speculate what the world would have been like if malaria had never evolved or spread. However, it seems reasonable to conclude that history would have been different.

5

Diagnosis and Treatment

DIAGNOSIS

Imagine someone going to a hospital emergency room with fever and severe headache. Physicians would perform the usual array of tests. Most of them, other than blood cell count, would probably come out normal. The physicians would most likely find this confusing. They might call on specialists for help. The patient's headaches might be a reason to call a neurologist, for example. Most American physicians would not begin to think to diagnose malaria, simply because they have never seen it. Consequently, someone who shows up in an American hospital emergency room with a case of malaria stands a great chance of being misdiagnosed. Of course, if the patient in question has recently been in a tropical country and the doctor thinks to ask about that, the odds of diagnosing malaria improve. There is still a good chance, however, that a diagnosis of malaria would not occur to most American physicians. Most have too little experience with the disease to suggest it.

One would think that the symptoms of malaria, including chills, fever, and blackwater urine, would be a good indication of the disease. However, there are a number of other diseases, such as severe nephritis, that could cause the same symptoms. The only way to positively diagnose malaria is by examining the patient's blood. A sample of blood is spread into a thin film on a glass slide, and the slide is examined under a microscope. If *Plasmodium* is found to be present in any of the blood cells, then malaria is confirmed.

There are other ways malaria can be diagnosed. For example, there is a "dipstick" method, in which a chemically sensitive strip of paper that detects parasite proteins is dipped in blood. There are other biochemical tests

Figure 5.1 The *Cinchona* tree, shown here, is the source for quinine. It is native to South America where the native peoples used an extract containing quinine to treat fever. Quinine can be found in the root, bark, and branches of the tree.

to detect parasite chemicals as well. The examination of blood films, however, remains the most accurate means of diagnosis.

TREATMENT

The first treatment of malaria was with quinine, a compound isolated from the bark of the *Cinchona* tree of South America (Figure 5.1). Sometimes it is still the most effective treatment available.

The first people to use *Cinchona* medically were the Indians of Peru, who used finely ground bark to treat fever. It was reasonable, therefore, for them to try to treat the fevers of malaria with ground cinchona bark. This treatment proved to be successful. Technically, quinine does not cure malaria because it does not kill all species of the parasite, but it kills enough of them to cure many people. Additionally, it does not kill at all stages of the *Plasmodium* life cycle. However, quinine can control the fevers of malaria and provide relief from the suffering. In certain areas, such as parts of South America, where newer malarial drugs are ineffective, unavailable, or too expensive, quinine is still used to treat malaria. Usually quinine

CINCHONA TREES

Cinchona trees are a genus of South American trees that belong to the family of plants known as the Rubiaceae, or madders. In the 1630s, Catholic missionaries in Peru observed the native people using bark from *Cinchona* trees to relieve fevers and as a muscle relaxant to relieve nighttime leg cramps. *Cinchona* trees were not known as a cure for malaria at the time because malaria was not yet recognized, if indeed it was present, in South America. Within ten years, the use of *Cinchona* trees to relieve fever had spread to Europe. Its eventual use in the treatment of malaria possibly resulted from first using it to relieve the fevers of malaria.

Quinine, the compound in *Cinchona* that is effective against malaria, is present in the root, branches, and bark of the tree. It is from the bark that quinine has traditionally been extracted and used medically. The bark was stripped off the trees and powdered. The use of *Cinchona* bark was so popular that trees were stripped without thought to conservation. Consequently, by the 1850s, the trees were becoming scarce and the price of the bark climbed. Perhaps pharmaceutical producers became concerned about extinction of the trees and the consequent loss of quinine to treat malaria. The trees

is given orally. In severe cases, where kidney failure or coma has occurred, it is given intravenously.

The first synthetic antimalarial medication was developed in Germany during the 1930s. It was called Atabrine. More medications were developed during World War II, as described below. These include Atabrine, chloroquine, doxycycline, and quinine, among others.

A number of antimalarial medications are used in combination with others. The treatment regimen varies according to the medication being used. For example, quinine, as quinine sulfate, is used in combination with the antibiotic doxycycline for seven days to treat *falciparum* malaria. It is effective, but

were subsequently introduced into Asia for cultivation, more likely for economic than conservationist reasons.

By 1820, scientists had learned how to extract quinine and cinchonine, another compound that is effective against malaria, from the bark rather than using powdered bark. This continued to be the practice during World War II, even though quinine had been synthesized by the 1930s. However, the Japanese occupation of the East Indies during the Second World War cut off the allies from their sources of quinine in Asia. Consequently, it became a matter of necessity that they developed synthetic medications for malaria.

Cinchona trees continue to grow in South America today. There are three major species of the tree. *Cinchona officinalis* grows in the Andes Mountains in Ecuador. *Cinchona calisaya* grows in Bolivia. *Cinchona succirubra* grows in Bolivia and Peru. Undoubtedly each species is not restricted to the country with which it is mentioned. There may be other species of *Cinchona* as well. Moreover, there are other types of trees from which quinine can be extracted. However, *Cinchona* has been the major source of quinine, and its impact on history cannot be denied.

causes a number of side effects, including hearing problems, nausea, and depression. A synthetic version of quinine, chloroquine, was developed and is now generally available. It is better tolerated than is quinine, but *Plasmodium* in some parts of the world have become resistant to it.

Alternatively, a medication called Malarone®, a commercial combination of drugs, can be used for three days. The drug

THE QUININE STORY

Quinine ($C_{20}H_{24}N_2O_2H_2O$) belongs in the category of chemicals known as alkaloids. Technically, it does not cure malaria because it does not kill *Plasmodium* in all stages of its life. However, it does kill it in a number of stages. It also relieves the fevers of malaria making it, at least, a viable treatment for malaria. Quinine naturally occurs in the bark, root, and branches of the *Cinchona* tree (*Cinchona calisaya* and *Cinchona succirubra*). These trees are found in the tropical forests of South America, particularly Bolivia, Peru, and Brazil. Native Americans in these tropical forests used *Cinchona* bark to treat fever by grinding the bark into a fine powder. Jesuit missionaries introduced *Cinchona* bark to Europe in the mid-seventeenth century. It turned out to be such a popular treatment for fever that the trees were routinely stripped of bark. Many trees died as a result. For a time, it appeared that the trees were endangered. If they had gone extinct, quinine might not be available today. The trees, however, were ultimately cultivated in Java, India, and Sri Lanka so the tree did not go extinct.

By the middle of the nineteenth century, chemists had learned how to extract the quinine from the bark, making the medicine easier to take. Since then, a number of synthetic forms of quinine have been developed. Many, such as chloroquine, are better tolerated by patients than is natural quinine.

In many areas of the world, *Plasmodium* has developed a resistance to chloroquine. Consequently, quinine is often still the drug of choice.

is effective, but very expensive. A third possibility is mefloquine for two days. The disadvantage of using mefloquine is that it causes severe stomach upset and has to be administered with a medication that prevents vomiting.

The impetus to develop synthetic anti-malarial drugs occurred during World War II, when the Japanese cut off the Allied supply of quinine from *Cinchona* after they conquered

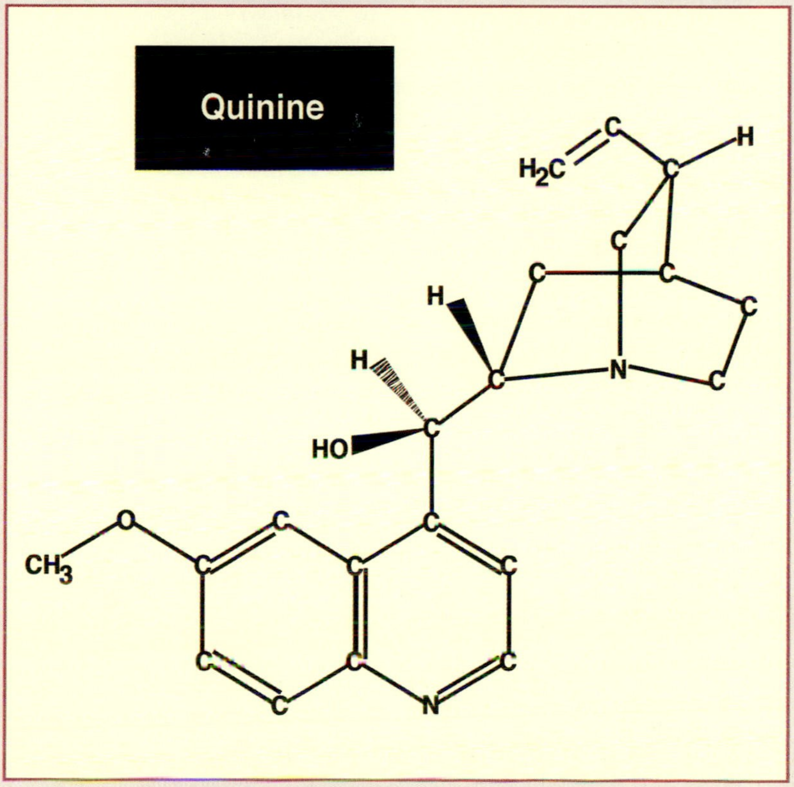

Quinine

Quinine, a compound isolated from the bark of the *Chinchona* tree, helps to alleviate the high fever associated with malaria. Quinine kills *Plasmodium* at some stages during its life cycle, but not all. Thus, it cannot be considered a true cure for the disease. The structure of quinine is shown here.

the South Pacific. Fortunately, chemists in Allied countries quickly developed synthetic substitutes.

Some of the medications that are used to treat malaria are also useful in preventing malaria (see Chapter 7). Unfortunately, some malaria medications are becoming less effective. The ineffectiveness of these medications may prove to be a problem in the future.

DRUG INEFFECTIVENESS

Any time we look at a group of people, we can easily identify differences among individuals. To *Plasmodium*, however, all people look pretty much alike. Similarly, any person looking at a culture of *Plasmodium* will not see much difference among individual parasites. Differences do exist, however. One difference is the susceptibility to various medications.

Plasmodium protozoa vary in their susceptibility to quinine. The variation in susceptibility can be explained as follows:

DOXYCYCLINE

Although doxycycline is effective in treating malaria, scientists are not certain how it works against the disease. Its principal use has been as a treatment for bacterial infections. Most antibacterial antibiotics, for example penicillin, ciprofloxine, and streptomycin, are ineffective against protozoa.

Doxycycline is part of the tetracycline group of antibiotics. It affects bacteria by interrupting protein synthesis, thus stopping their growth and allowing body defenses to work against them. It is also effective against a number of infections, including Lyme disease, some gastrointestinal disorders, and urinary tract infections.

There are a few disadvantages to using doxycycline, however. For example, it can cause discoloration of teeth in growing children. Additionally, it can cause gastrointestinal distress, such as diarrhea and nausea. It can also cause headaches, skin itching, and sensitivity to light.

Suppose enough quinine is added to a culture of *Plasmodium* to kill 99 percent of the parasites. The surviving organisms are less susceptible to the antibiotic than the ones that died. The survivors are then allowed to reproduce until their numbers equal those in the original culture. It is likely that the survivors would pass their resistance on to their offspring. It is also possible that gene mutations would occur that might make one individual even more resistant to the drug. This mutant would then pass on its resistance. Consequently, although the same amount of quinine that killed 99 percent of the original culture might not leave the newer culture untouched, it would kill fewer than it did in the original. The mutant individuals would require an even stronger preparation of quinine to be killed. This resistance can happen when a patient is given too little of an antibiotic, the patient does not take all of the medication, or the treatment is too short to kill the entire parasite population. The drug will selectively allow resistant members to survive and pass on their resistance. Several rounds of this can end up leading to the evolution of totally resistant parasites. This situation has happened with bacteria that have become resistant to drugs like penicillin. It is also happening with *Plasmodium* that are becoming resistant to quinine, chloroquine, and other antimalarial medications. Indeed, in Africa, India, and Southeast Asia, most strains of *falciparum* malaria are resistant to chloroquine. Worse, in Cambodia and Thailand, there are some types of *falciparum* that appear to be resistant to all antimalarial drugs.

HERBAL TREATMENT

Recently, there has been a lot of interest in herbal medicines. By definition, an herbal medication is one that is extracted from a plant. For example, a daisy-like plant by the name of *Echinacea* has been found to be effective in shortening the duration and reducing the intensity of the common cold. Another plant, the saw palmetto, common to the southeast, has been shown to be beneficial for male urinary health.

By that definition, quinine could be considered to be an herbal medication because it was isolated from a tree. In general, herbal medicines are not commonly used in the United States. Elsewhere, such as in China, for example, herbal medicines are used to treat malaria. One herb that is particularly effective is a compound known as artemisinin or sometimes artesunate. It is isolated from the leaves of the sweet wormwood plant *Artemisia annua* (Figure 5.2), and it appears to be toxic to *Plasmodium*.

Artemisinin has been used medically in China for centuries. It was recently tested for effectiveness against *falciparum* malaria in Thailand, where malaria was becoming resistant to mefloquine, a historically effective drug. When artemisinin and mefloquine were given together to patients, the cure rate was 100 percent. Furthermore, since artemisinin has been used, mefloquine has increased in effectiveness. Oddly enough, there have been several cases where artemisinin used in combination with standard drug therapies, such as quinine, has been shown to be very effective in treating malaria.

Artemisinin is available in China and Europe. It has not been approved for use in the United States partly because it is highly toxic to people. Because malaria is not a problem in the United States, however, the toxicity is no cause for concern. One might ask, however, why something that is toxic would be used on people at all. The answer is that many drugs, in excess, are toxic to people. Cancer chemotherapeutics, for example, work because they are toxic. This toxicity explains why so many people have adverse reactions to cancer drugs, such as nausea and hair loss. Because cancer cells are metabolically faster than normal tissue, they absorb the chemotherapeutic agent more rapidly, thus getting poisoned in the process. Likewise, a medication such as artemisinin can be effective against a disease, even if it is toxic to the victim. The small amount of artemisinin needed to kill malaria parasites in an infected person is much less than is necessary to kill the person who carries the parasites. Artemisinin could still make the patient

Figure 5.2 Certain herbal treatments can be used to reduce the symptoms of malaria. Chinese Sweet Wormwood, shown here, has been used effectively in China and Thailand. It is also available in Europe but has not been approved for use in the United States.

ill. The theory is that the temporary illness caused by taking a potentially poisonous medicine is preferable to having and possibly dying from a disease.

Even with medicines for treatment available, malaria can still be extremely debilitating. In extreme cases, patients with *falciparum* malaria have to be hospitalized and, in some cases, given antibiotics and fluids intravenously. In serious cases, patients have to have blood transfusions, kidney dialysis, and breathing assistance. Indeed, the effect of malaria on one's body can be so severe, it can actually make the body inhospitable to other infections.

6

Attempts at Malarial Control

After the attack on the World Trade Center on September 11, 2001, the vulnerability of the United States to terrorists has become a reality to millions of people. Although most people do not worry about hijacked airplanes being flown into their houses, many worry about **bioterrorism**. The thought of receiving an anthrax-laden letter had people petrified for months. Indeed, letters contaminated with anthrax were sent to a newspaper and television studios. Some postal workers who handled such letters developed the disease, and a few of them died. There was a lot of talk about anthrax as a weapon, as there was about smallpox and perhaps botulism. There was also an attempt to release a culture of disease organisms into a Tokyo subway by a cult group in Japan, and a possible terrorist cell was discovered in England in the process of manufacturing ricin, a deadly poison isolated from the castor bean plant.

No one seems to be trying to use malaria as a **bioweapon**. Unlike the diseases that are most feared in biological warfare, malaria cannot be grown easily in culture. Malaria requires living hosts in which to grow, and those hosts must be human. Malaria that affects humans cannot be grown in laboratory animals. Secondly, because there is no way malaria could be spread from person to person by either direct contact or by contaminated media, the logistics of distributing the disease throughout a susceptible population render it impossible. Malaria requires the mosquito vector. Consequently, despite the devastation malaria has caused on humans throughout history, it cannot be used as a weapon.

Characteristics that render malaria ineffective as a weapon, such as the fact that it is not contagious, are also points of vulnerability that can be exploited in dealing with the disease. Infected patients can be treated with medication to cure them, as is the case with most other infections. Additionally, because malaria is completely dependent upon the *Anopheles* mosquito as a vector, and because the life cycle of that vector is well known and understood, it can be disrupted to prevent transfer of the disease among susceptible people. In short, to eliminate malaria, one might declare war on the mosquitoes that spread it.

THE WAR AGAINST MOSQUITOES

To fight a war effectively, one must know one's enemy. In the case of the *Anopheles* mosquito, scientists know a lot. In fact, once the relationship between the mosquito and the *Plasmodium* parasites became understood, it became evident that eliminating the mosquito alternative host and vector would eliminate the disease.

The *Anopheles* mosquito has a two-part life cycle: an aquatic larval and pupal stage and a terrestrial adult stage, during which it spreads malaria. During its larval stage, the *Anopheles* mosquito is strongly tied to the surface of the water in which it lives, more so, in fact, than other genera of mosquitoes. That is perhaps the most vulnerable part of the mosquito's life, and it was how the war against them was initially fought. In most areas where this was done successfully, malaria was brought under control.

DESTROYING THE ENEMY'S HOMELAND

Mosquitoes require standing water to reproduce. Therefore, eliminating standing water is a major step in controlling mosquitoes. This action turned out to be part of several successful highly integrated attempts to deal with malaria.

For example, malaria had been a problem in Italy since the time of the Romans. It was brought under control, in part, during the dictatorship of Benito Mussolini, between World Wars I and II. Mussolini instituted a program to drain the swamps in which the mosquitoes were breeding. In Havana, Cuba, William C. Gorgas, a United States Army physician who had previously helped bring malaria and yellow fever under control in the Panama canal, practically eliminated malaria by larval control, including drainage of breeding sites. In the United States, drainage of swamps and clearing land for agriculture and other use contributed to the elimination of malaria.

Ironically, in the Tennessee River watershed, despite the fact that most freely flowing rivers were channelized and dammed to form large reservoirs for navigation and power generation, malaria did not spread. The common *Anopheles* mosquito in the region, *Anopheles quadrimaculatus*, breeds along the margins of large bodies of water. It would seem that the reservoirs should have provided a perfect location for breeding. However, the practice of letting water out of the reservoirs to maintain flow in the rivers left mosquito larvae stranded in small puddles, where they died as the puddles dried.

THE SECOND FRONT—CHEMICAL WARFARE

Physical elimination of mosquito breeding grounds, although effective, was not always practical. Cities did not want the ponds in their parks drained, for example. Consequently, a second front in the war was necessary. The front came in the form of the insecticide "Paris green."

Paris green (cupric acetoarsenite, $C_4H_6As_6Cu_4O_{16}$), is an organic, copper salt of the element arsenic, a known poison. It was first used in 1867 to control the Colorado potato beetle. In 1920, it was dispersed by airplanes in the swamps of Louisiana against mosquitoes. In many respects, Paris green is ideal for dealing with mosquito larvae, particularly *Anopheles* larvae. Paris green is not soluble in water. It has to be dissolved in kerosene to be sprayed. The solution floats on the surface where *Anopheles* larvae feed. Consequently, the larvae are exposed to the poison, but the animals that live within the water are not. In particular, the small amounts that are effective against the mosquito larvae appear to have no impact on fish and wildlife, including fish that eat mosquito larvae. However, it is difficult to believe that the kerosene in which Paris green is dissolved is harmless.

INSECTICIDES

Insecticides, by definition, are poisons that are used specifically to kill insects, just as fungicides are used on fungal pests and herbicides are used on weeds. Paris green and **DDT** are only two of thousands of different chemicals used to kill insect pests. Many insecticides are natural, or organic, in the popular sense. For example, pyrethrum, which is isolated from chrysanthemums, is an effective insecticide. Rotenone is isolated from the roots of a certain tropical tree. Natural insecticides often are biodegradable, which means they are naturally broken down by microorganisms and must be reapplied frequently. Even nicotine, a natural product of tobacco leaves that has been associated with the harmful effects of smoking, has been used as a natural insecticide. Synthetic **pesticides**, in contrast, are often persistent—they remain effective for weeks or months after they are applied.

DDT is part of a family of synthetic insecticides called the chlorinated hydrocarbons, which also includes chlordane and toxaphene. These are particularly persistent chemicals—that is, they do not degrade in nature, and their residues can accumulate in animal tissues. The other major family of synthetics is the organophosphates, which include Malathion and Parathion. These are also effective insecticides; but, unlike the chlorinated hydrocarbons, they do readily degrade. For example, more than 50 percent of the Malathion that is applied to a field of sandy soil may break down overnight. Consequently, organophosphates must be applied more frequently.

Paris green was used in the United States in standing water that could not be drained. It contributed significantly to the elimination of malaria. It was effective elsewhere as well, for example in Egypt and Brazil, where *falciparum* malaria was causing problems. Paris green was also part of Mussolini's war against mosquitoes in Italy. After World War II, Paris green was replaced by other compounds, including one that chemists of the time believed to be a chemical miracle: DDT.

DDT ($C_{14}H_9Cl_5$) or dichloro-diphenyl-trichloroethane, is a member of the family of organic chemicals known as the chlorinated hydrocarbons (Figure 6.1). It was invented by Othmar Zieller, a German pharmacist, in 1874. Paul Hermann Müller, a Swiss chemist, experimentally exposed mosquitoes to DDT. In 1939, he showed how effective it was against insects. In 1948, Müller was awarded a Nobel Prize for his discovery.

DDT was very effective in killing insects, including mosquitoes and other disease vectors. It appeared to be harmless to people. It was first used during World War II when it was sprayed in the South Pacific to control malaria. Given the problem malaria presented to American troops, one can only imagine what the war would have been like had the chemical not been used. DDT was also used in Europe to kill typhus-carrying lice. After the war, it was used extensively in agriculture to combat plant pests as well as in disease control. In India, it reduced malaria incidence from 75 million cases to fewer than 5 million during a ten-year period. DDT did not just kill insects on contact, it remained active in soil or on plants, killing weeks, even months, after it was applied.

DDT may have been too effective. In many cases, it was abused. By the late 1940s, DDT was sprayed regularly on trees (Figure 6.2) to kill not only mosquitoes, but also tree pests and other irritating insects. There was no danger from

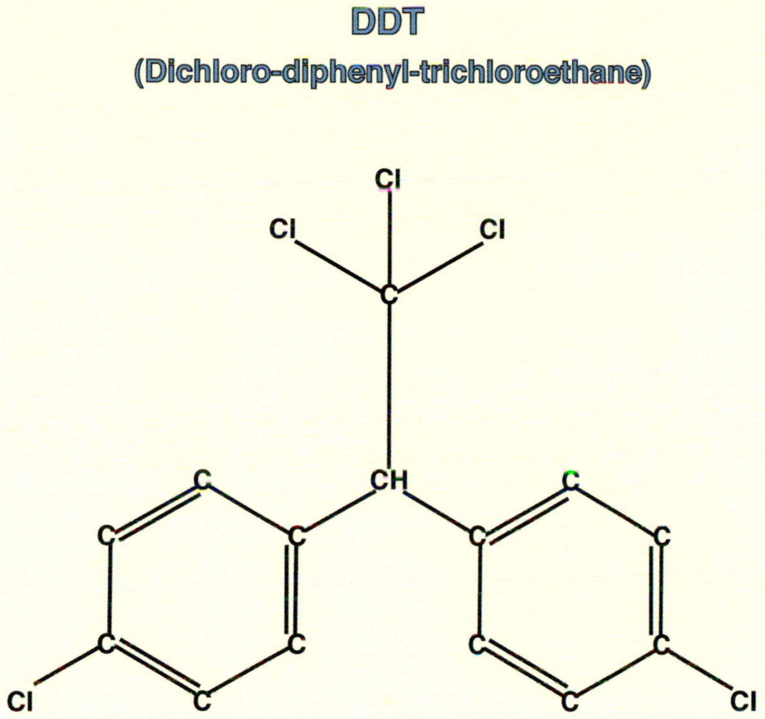

DDT

(Dichloro-diphenyl-trichloroethane)

Figure 6.1 Insecticides are often very effective in the short term, but can prove very dangerous to the environment in the long term. Furthermore, insects can develop resistance to insecticides, and either the chemicals stop working or a higher and higher dose is needed to retain their insecticidal properties. DDT (dichloro-diphenyl-trichloroethane), shown here, was a very popular insecticide that was used during World War II against mosquitoes. However, it can remain active in the soil and in the bodies of animals for months, and it can be transferred through the food chain until it accumulates to fatal levels in an animal.

Figure 6.2 Spraying trees with chemicals such as DDT was very popular in the 1950s. In this picture, field workers spray trees in Connecticut after a flood in 1955. While insecticides may have temporarily helped the mosquito problem, people were unaware of its devastating effects on wildlife.

malaria, yellow fever, or any other insect-borne disease: it was sprayed to make life more comfortable. DDT was packaged in aerosol cans to kill houseflies. It was used liberally on farms to kill animal pests.

In the 1950s, problems with DDT began to accumulate. Because it did not degrade into harmless substances in the environment, DDT could migrate from its point of application out to forests and waterways. Here, it entered the natural food chain and accumulated in the tissues of animals and even people.

Second, DDT is a nonselective poison. It kills not only its target insects, but others as well. DDT killed beneficial insects such as bees, butterflies, and other pollinating and predatory insects such as dragonflies and praying mantises that ate insect pests. It also killed insects and other small animals such as worms upon which birds fed. Thirdly, its effectiveness against pests began to wane as the more susceptible members of insect pests species were eliminated and more resistant ones survived.

The old expression, "Anything that seems too good to be true probably is," can be applied to DDT. Even Paul Hermann Müller worried about the future effects of DDT. In 1962, marine biologist Rachel Carson published *Silent Spring*, a book in which she documented the growing environmental threat that DDT was presenting. Carson has often been credited as the individual around whom the environmental movement of the 1960s began. In reality, there were a number of important contributors to the environmental movement. However, Carson's book encouraged people to question the safety and effectiveness of DDT.

Research on the threats of DDT supported many of the claims made against the pesticide. By 1973, DDT spraying in the United States was banned. The decision did not sit well with all of America. The petrochemical industry that produced DDT was not pleased that a profitable product had been outlawed, farmers were concerned that their productivity would decline, and public health officials worried about epidemics of vector-borne diseases reoccurring.

This was not an empty worry. Indeed, there has been an increase in the frequency of malaria in parts of the world, particularly Africa, in recent years, and many health

(continued on page 66)

BIOACCUMULATION

In addition to being synthetic, DDT is fat-soluble. If a mosquito absorbs some DDT, too little to kill it, the animal's body cannot break down the chemical. Instead, the DDT is absorbed into the animal's fat, where it remains. A dragonfly that eats the mosquito would then acquire the DDT from the mosquito. The dragonfly would be unable to break down the DDT, which would be stored in its fat, as would any DDT in all of the mosquitoes the dragonfly ate. If a fish eats the dragonfly, the DDT gets stored in the fish's fat, as does the DDT in all of the bugs and smaller animals the fish eats. In this way, DDT gets concentrated in fatty tissue as it is passed through a food chain, a string of one animal eating another. By the time an osprey eats the fish, it is getting a pretty concentrated dose of DDT. If the osprey eats enough contaminated fish, it may accumulate enough DDT to cause internal harm.

DDT causes substantial damage in the reproductive systems of birds. It disrupts the series of reactions that put calcium into the shells of the eggs that birds produce. Thus, birds that have been exposed to high amounts of DDT may produce eggs with very thin shells (Figure 6.3), which easily break, or eggs with no shells at all. Baby birds cannot develop in such eggs and die.

DDT can accumulate in people as well. Farm workers who are exposed to the chemical may end up with it in their tissues, as can people who eat a lot of contaminated fish. In people, DDT often ends up in the liver and in fatty tissue, including the mammary tissue of women's breasts. In women who are lactating (producing milk), DDT can be passed on to their babies when they nurse.

There is no conclusive evidence that DDT is harmful to people. But DDT has been shown to cause cancer in laboratory animals; therefore, it is potentially cancerous for humans as well. Furthermore, because DDT kills some animals and interrupts the reproductive systems of others, it could possibly harm people as well.

Other harmful environmental contaminants called polychlorinated biphenyls (PCBs) are chemically similar to DDT. The two chemicals can be confused during testing. Consequently, it is sometimes difficult to know which one, if not both, is present. PCBs cause identifiable problems in animals that receive a large enough dose. Scientists are fairly certain that PCBs can harm humans.

Figure 6.3 *DDT can accumulate in the bodies of animals, causing severe problems and even death. In birds, DDT accumulation causes weakened or broken eggshells, in which baby birds cannot survive. Examples of DDT-affected eggs are shown here (the picture is tinted green for better visibility).*

(continued from page 63)

authorities would like to see DDT used again. However, it is questionable that the ban on DDT is responsible for the resurgence of malaria or any other vector-borne disease. Many countries outside of the United States, including several that export produce to the United States, continue to use DDT. Many countries where malaria occurs also use DDT. It is likely that the recent increases in malaria cases are more due to the resistance of mosquitoes to DDT and the resistance of *Plasmodium* protozoa to antimalarial medications than from the DDT ban.

THE THIRD FRONT—PHYSICAL WARFARE

Destroying mosquito breeding grounds and poisoning insects accomplished much in terms of controlling malaria, but other methods were applied as well. In rural areas, for example, water that accumulated in abandoned tires became mosquito breeding grounds. Proper disposal of the tires, and anything else in which water could collect, reduced mosquitoes' opportunities to breed. In addition, putting screens on windows prevented mosquitoes from biting people. Screening windows did not reduce the number of mosquitoes, but it probably forced mosquitoes to find other victims, animals in

DDT RESISTANCE

In the previous chapter, the problem with drug resistance in malaria protozoa was described. The same mechanism applies to mosquitoes and DDT. Some mosquitoes are naturally resistant to the poison. For reasons that are not understood, some mosquitoes have experienced gene mutations that allow them to decompose DDT. Gene mutations can also increase the resistance of a population of mosquitoes over time, especially as DDT selectively eliminates the more susceptible members. This resistance has already occurred.

particular, in which the *Plasmodium* protozoan could not survive. Malaria was wiped out in the United States because of the combination of actions used against them: drainage, pesticides, and window screens. Treatment with medications, as described in the previous chapter, also contributed significantly to eliminating malaria. Although some mosquitoes managed to survive, reproduce, find victims, and become resistant to pesticides, the absence of disease reservoirs meant that malaria could not be spread.

7
Preventing Malaria

AVOIDING THE BITE

To get malaria, a person must be bitten by a malaria-infected mosquito.
The best way to avoid getting bitten by a mosquito is to avoid mosquitoes
entirely. Doing that requires knowledge of the mosquito's behavior and
adjusting one's own behavior to compensate. For example, mosquitoes are
most active at dusk and dawn, so avoiding outdoor activity at those
times limits exposure to the insect. Additionally, mosquitoes are
able to "see" heat. Sense organs on their antennae detect infrared
light, which our bodies radiate when we shed heat. Wearing protective
clothing, particularly light colored clothing that radiates infrared light
much less than darker clothes, helps to avoid a mosquito's bite.

ELIMINATING BREEDING GROUNDS

Other means of avoiding mosquitoes involve limiting their opportunities
to breed and find you when you are vulnerable. In the previous chapter,
it was mentioned that abandoned tires collect rainwater and provide
ideal locations where mosquitoes can breed. Mosquitoes can also breed in
swimming pools, birdbaths, fountains, animal watering troughs, roof
gutters, and even in carelessly discarded cans and beverage containers.
Denying mosquitoes' access to such objects, by keeping them dry
whenever possible, or removing litter, limits the opportunities of
mosquitoes to reproduce. In cases where water must stand, as in
swimming pools, chemicals, such as chlorine, can be added to the
water to kill mosquito larvae. In some cases, mosquito fish (*Gambusia
affinis*) can be introduced into water. These are small fish that eat
mosquito larvae.

USING PROTECTIVE BARRIERS

Barriers to mosquitoes, such as window screens and bed nets can also be effective in limiting mosquitoes' opportunities to find victims. Bed nets can be impregnated with chemicals that repel mosquitoes which make them even more effective at protecting against the insects (Figures 7.1 and 7.2).

USING REPELLANTS

Sometimes, however, mosquitoes simply cannot be avoided. Certain areas such as deep woods or swamps have mosquito populations that may be so dense and/or hungry the mosquitos

MOSQUITO FISH

Mosquito fish (*Gambusia affinis*) are semitropical fish that were originally native to the southeastern United States, Central America, and the Caribbean. They are live-bearing fish, which means that they give birth to living young rather than laying eggs that hatch later, like most fish. They are similar to and related to the guppy. In nature, mosquito fish grow larger than the guppy. Males reach a length of one to two inches, but females can grow up to twice that length. Mosquito fish prefer quiet waters more than rapidly flowing streams and rivers. The fish feed voraciously on mosquito larvae or other small aquatic invertebrates. Because of their affinity for mosquito larvae, mosquito fish have been transplanted across much of the world, particularly into areas where malaria is a problem.

Unfortunately, there are disadvantages to introducing mosquito fish into areas where they are not native. Mosquito fish tend to eat the larvae of other fishes, as well as tadpoles of tree frogs and aquatic insects, in addition to mosquito larvae. Mosquito fish are best used to control mosquito populations in isolated ponds and ditches.

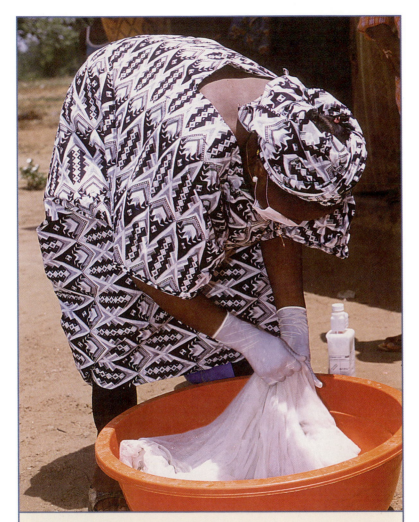

Figure 7.1 Using protective barriers, such as screens and mosquito nets, can help guard against mosquito bites. Often, mosquito nets are coated in mosquito repellants and hung over beds. The woman in this picture is washing her mosquito net in a chemical repellant solution.

may be active at all hours, including in bright sunlight. More-over, there are times when people have to be out at dusk or dawn. In such cases, chemical mosquito repellents can be used to prevent bites.

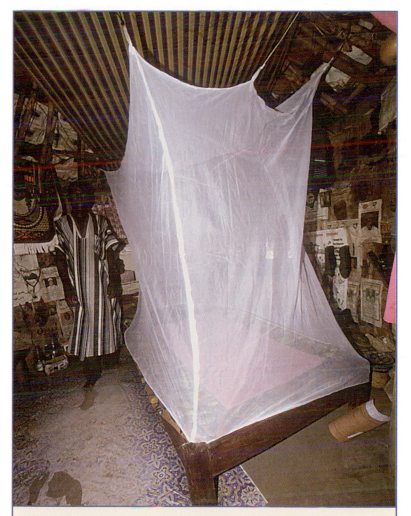

Figure 7.2 Mosquito nets have greatly reduced the incidences of malaria, particularly in Africa. This man stands by a bed which is covered with such a net that protects him from biting mosquitoes during the night.

Everybody has had the experience of coming across a smell that is so putrid that he or she wants to get far away from it as quickly as possible. Ideally, that is what a good insect repellent does to mosquitoes. The repellant makes the person who is wearing it seem too unappealing to bite. Additionally, a good repellant must be harmless to people, must not be washed away by perspiration or water, and must be long lasting so that it does not have to be reapplied frequently.

One material that is popularly used as a mosquito repellent is Skin-So-Soft®, a bath oil, which is marketed by Avon Products, Inc. Although it is not intended to be a mosquito repellent, it does seem to work as one, probably because its odor is offensive to mosquitoes. In one respect, it is ideal: it is not harmful. However, this product apparently evaporates from the skin and does not protect for very long. Permethrin (a potent insecticide), in contrast, is effective for a long time, but is too toxic to be applied directly to skin or to clothing. However, it can be impregnated into bed nets. The most effective mosquito repellents are those that contain the compound known as DEET.

Known chemically as N, N-diethyl-meta-toluamide, DEET ($C_{12}H_{17}NO$) is perhaps the most effective commercially available mosquito repellent available today. It is long lasting and generally not harmful, if it is used properly. It should not be used in concentrations of more than 50 percent for adults and 10 percent for children under two years of age. The safest and most effective concentration is between 15 and 30 percent. DEET can be applied to skin or to clothing. Excessive amounts can cause skin irritation. It can also cause irritation to the cornea if it gets in the eye. It can irritate the mucus membranes of the mouth or nose if it comes into contact with them.

DEET is present in most commercially familiar insect repellents, such as Off® or Cutter®. It is not harmful if it is used only on skin, not moist tissues, and it is not used in large concentrations. Moreover, DEET is long lasting. A single application of a DEET-containing repellent can keep mosquitoes away for several hours.

There are some traditional means of repelling mosquitoes that have questionable effectiveness. For example, massive amounts of vitamin B_1 (thiamine) supposedly repel mosquitoes. When supplied with excesses of the vitamin, the body will use whatever it needs and excrete the excess through the pores. Some people claim that using this has kept mosquitoes away from them; others claim it does nothing. Vitamin B_1 excess is not known to be harmful, but taking too much of any substance is not recommended without a doctor's advice. Similarly, garlic is said to repel mosquitoes if consumed in sufficient amounts. It too is excreted through the pores. Although it may or may not work against mosquitoes, too much of it will keep people away.

A CASE HISTORY: BURUNDI

Burundi is a small country in central Africa just south of the equator, west of Tanzania and north of Lake Tanganyika. It is a poor country, one that has been torn by political strife in the past and now suffers from a very high incidence of AIDS. As with much of tropical Africa, Burundi also suffers from a high incidence of *falciparum* malaria. In the autumn of 2000, Burundi was experiencing 300 deaths per month. Moreover, the malaria parasites in Burundi have become highly resistant to chloroquine and a combination of sulfadoxine and pyrimethamine, the usual drugs of choice for treating malaria in Africa. Since 2000, with the financial support of the World Health Organization and UNICEF, Burundi has adopted a promising way to treat malaria. The treatment involves a rapid treatment of malaria (i.e., within 24 hours of symptom onset), and uses a combination of artesunate and amodiaquine. This treatment regimen is reported to be more than 95 percent effective.

MALARIA PROPHYLAXIS

Medically speaking, the term *prophylaxis* means prevention. Thus getting a flu shot is an example of a prophylactic act. At the moment, a vaccine does not exist that will prevent malaria, but several medications that are used to treat malaria are also effective in preventing it. Malaria prophylaxis is usually given to somebody who is not normally exposed to malaria, but is going to be traveling in an area where malaria is present.

Many of the medications that are used to treat malaria are also effective in preventing it. These drugs are usually given to somebody who will be traveling into an area where malaria is a risk. The patient starts taking the medication before he or she begins the trip and continues for a while after he or she returns. The exact regimen depends upon the specific drug prescribed.

In the case of chloroquine, where it is still effective, the patient begins taking the drug one week before the trip and continues for four weeks afterward, usually taking one pill each week. The same is true for mefloquine. Doxycycline is taken daily. It can be started one or two days before travel and can be continued for four weeks after return. Malarone® is also taken beginning two days before travel. It is taken daily and continued for one week once the trip is over.

Malaria medications can cause some undesirable side effects, including upset stomach and severe vomiting. Over an extended period of time, these side effects could cause dehydration.

ROLL BACK MALARIA

Because malaria is a global problem, the best solution is also likely to be global. "Roll Back Malaria" (RBM), a global partnership jointly founded by the World Health Organization, the United Nations Development Programme, UNICEF, and the World Bank in 1998, was started in Africa, where malaria is at its worst. The program includes national governments, research institutions, private organizations, professional societies, United Nations and developmental agencies, and the media. The goal of the program is to reduce the frequency of malaria by half by the year 2010. It addresses the problem of malaria in several ways, including prevention and treatment. Prevention involves using pesticide-impregnated bed nets.

The treatment involves medications using intelligence-based interventions, which means using geographic information systems to apply drugs and insecticides only where they are effective and needed. If, for example, the *Plasmodium* in a particular region of Africa is resistant to chloroquine, it would be senseless to use chloroquine; some other medication would have to be used. The drug treatment is given in a clinical setting, using whatever drug or drug combination is effective in that area. The program also wants to expand the use of effective treatments and to respond rapidly whenever an outbreak occurs. A particularly important target for both prevention and treatment is pregnant women, because malaria can fatally harm both the mother and her unborn child. The program does not call for widespread spraying of pesticides to kill mosquitoes, because that has been shown to be ineffective in the long term.

A third part of the program is the support of research for better treatments. This endeavor includes a subprogram called Medicines for Malaria Venture (MMV), which works to raise money for the support of new drug development. The program's initial target was to raise $15 million by 2001. The group eventually wants to raise $30 million per year. A long-term goal is to become self-supporting by selling drugs that were developed with program support. MMV hopes to accomplish this goal by 2010.

8

Malaria Now

If Sir Alexander Fleming, the British scientist who discovered penicillin, were alive today, he would probably be astonished to find out that his discovery was now ineffective in combating many of the disease germs that it easily wiped out at the time of his death. Likewise, if William C. Gorgas, the U.S. Army physician who helped in the control of malaria and yellow fever in Panama and nearly wiped out malaria in Cuba, were to return today, he would most likely also be astonished to learn that the disease has not been brought under control worldwide. The reality is, however, that over most of the world, malaria is as much of a problem now as it was 50 years ago, or perhaps even worse (Figure 8.1). Today, some mosquitoes are resistant to DDT, and some varieties of *Plasmodium* are resistant to certain medications.

There have been some successes in the war against malaria. The disease is no longer a problem in North America, Europe, much (but not all) of Central America, and many islands in the South Pacific. It is also not nearly the problem in South America that it once was. Otherwise, however, malaria is present over much of the world. In fact, malaria, tuberculosis (a bacterial infection of the lungs), and schistosomiasis (a disease caused by a parasitic worm), in combination, kill more people worldwide than any other combination of three diseases (Figure 8.2). Of the three, only tuberculosis appears to be a current threat in the United States. Schistosomiasis most probably will never occur in the United States because to complete its life cycle it requires a species of snail that cannot live there. Malaria has occurred in the United States in the past, and it could return.

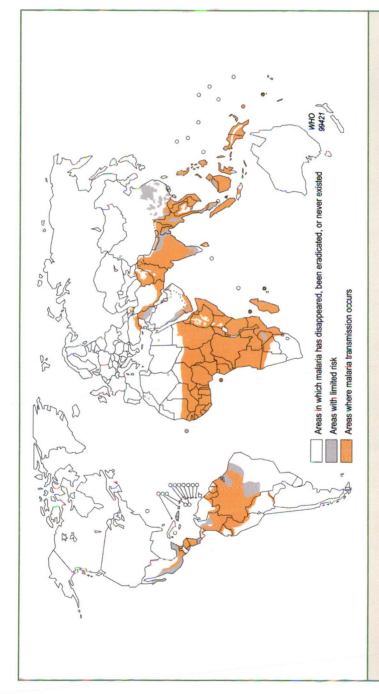

Figure 8.1 Malaria is most prevalent in northern South America, Africa, and India. However, malaria can become a worldwide problem if the *Plasmodium* parasite is carried to an uninfected area of the world, either in a mosquito or a human, and spread among other mosquitoes in that area.

Areas in which malaria has disappeared, been eradicated, or never existed

Areas with limited risk

Areas where malaria transmission occurs

WHO
99421

THE LEADING INFECTIOUS CAUSES OF DEATH WORLDWIDE, 2000

Lower respiratory infections	3.9 million
HIV/AIDS	2.9 million
Diarrheal diseases	2.1 million
Tuberculosis	1.7 million
Malaria	1.1 million
Measles	777,000

Figure 8.2 As of 2002, malaria was one of the leading causes of death by an infectious disease worldwide. HIV/AIDS tops the list as the biggest deadly disease, with malaria appearing fourth. It caused 1.1 million deaths in the year 2000.

IN AFRICA

Although some of the worst malarial drug resistance is in Asia, most cases of malaria are occurring in Africa. About 80 percent of the world's malaria exists in Africa. As in the past, its persistence is facilitated by the behavior of the people who live there. In the African countries of Ethiopia and Namibia, for example, people use soil to make mud bricks, which they use in constructing their homes. The activity leaves pits in the soil that can fill with water in which the common mosquito of the region, *Anopheles gambiae*, breeds. Most species of *Anopheles* thrive better in large bodies of water, unlike *Anopheles gambiae*. Because the people of the region are farmers that grow corn, mosquito larvae feed on corn pollen that lands on the water. Once they become adults, the mosquitoes are able to travel over a distance of about two miles, about 3.2 kilometers, from their breeding sites. People living within that area become the mosquitoes' victims.

It may seem that the situation could easily be controlled if the Namibian and Ethiopian people could be persuaded to find other means of building their homes. However, the behavior pattern is perhaps one that is culturally engrained, and changing such a pattern is not easy. In addition, there are precious few resources in the region. Mud bricks are sometimes the only material available for home construction. Moreover, there is a lot of poverty and rapid population growth in both countries, two factors that complicate matters. If other materials were available for home construction, most of the people may not be able to afford them.

A POTENTIAL WORLDWIDE THREAT

Although malaria mostly affects Asia and Africa at the moment, it can potentially erupt into a worldwide problem very quickly. There are several reasons why this could happen. First, Americans and Europeans travel to areas with malaria rather regularly. **Ecotourism**, the travel to natural environments like rain forests, has become extremely popular and many people expose themselves to tropical diseases. About 30,000 Americans and Europeans become infected with malaria every year because of travel. If these people return home unaware of their infections and *Anopheles* mosquitoes are around, there is a real risk that malaria will be spread. Indeed, epidemics can be started this way.

In 2002, a couple of cases of malaria showed up in the Washington, D.C., area. These were probably people who had been traveling abroad. Because Washington, D.C., is densely populated and is also a popular tourist destination, the potential

MALARIA AND GLOBAL WARMING

Global warming is the worldwide increase in average annual temperature. For the past 100 years or more, the world has been becoming a warmer place. It is believed by many, including scientists, that humans are the cause of global warming.

Carbon dioxide, the gas that is given off as a result of combustion, acts something like a blanket in that it prevents heat from escaping from the earth. Since the industrial revolution, the burning of fossil fuel has increased the amount of carbon dioxide in the atmosphere and, therefore, increased the global temperature. Glaciers are melting faster than they are growing, the polar ice caps are thinning, and many species of plants and animals that live in the temperate regions of the world are extending their ranges into what have historically been colder climates. Additionally, some island nations, such as the Maldives and Seychelles in the Indian Ocean, have expressed concern that global warming has increased the sea level and is threatening their shorelines. The exact cause of the increasing temperatures worldwide is still under debate. Theoretically, the increase in temperature should exacerbate the risk of malaria spreading around the world because malaria is largely a tropical disease and *falciparum* malaria is almost entirely tropical. In theory, as world temperatures increase, the range of malaria would conceivably become larger.

To date, there is no evidence that global warming has affected the distribution of malaria. In fact, the recent increases in malaria cases have been linked to population growth and poverty. However, if the climate continues to warm, it may contribute to the spread of malaria in the future.

for malaria to spread rapidly was present. Because people from Washington, D.C., travel all over the country and over the world, a malaria outbreak in Washington, D.C., could easily spread to other places.

The ease of long distance travel, along with the short incubation period of malaria, makes it possible for malaria to be spread rapidly. Complicating the problem is the reality that most European and American physicians, as suggested in Chapter 5, do not deal with malaria on a regular basis. Many of them would not recognize the symptoms right away. Consequently, somebody who is seeking treatment for malaria in Europe or the United States could be easily misdiagnosed and treated for the wrong disease.

Also possible, although much less likely, is that an infected mosquito could fly into the open cargo bay of an airliner in, say, the Philippines, sit on a wall, and fly out the next day when the plane is being unloaded in Los Angeles. It has been suggested that West Nile virus made its way from the Middle East to New York this way. Indeed, malaria spread from Africa to South America by mosquitoes hitching rides on fast mail boats a century ago. Malaria would be more easily contained than West Nile, which infects birds as well as people, but malaria can be more serious.

Malaria could conceivably spread across the world once more. This time, however, it will be caused by *Plasmodium* that are resistant to antibiotics. It may be spread by mosquitoes that are resistant to DDT. Moreover, global warming, a growing environmental concern, has the potential to make the problem even worse (see box on previous page).

9
The Future of Malaria

In 1898, English author Herbert George (H.G.) Wells published his science fiction novel *The War of the Worlds.* In his book, an invasion from Mars was ultimately thwarted by the Earth's bacteria. The Martians, a technologically advanced civilization, had long since eliminated all lower forms of life from their planet, including **pathogenic** bacteria and other parasites. With no challenges, the Martians' immune systems degenerated. Upon being exposed to bacteria during their invasion of Earth, their immune systems failed to protect them and they died. The story is probably better known from Orson Welles' radio broadcast in 1938. The broadcast was so realistic that tens of thousands of people actually believed that the Earth was being invaded by aliens.

The theory behind H.G. Wells' story was faulty, of course. Many of the microorganisms with which we share our planet are essential for our existence. Eliminating them would cause our own extinction. It is extremely likely that eliminating bacteria would also eliminate all other forms of life on any other planet where life exists, if there are any. Still, many believe that as technology advances, humans will gain more control over biology, perhaps to the point where diseases and the organisms that cause them may be eliminated.

Currently, 10 percent of the world population has malaria. Every twelve seconds a child dies from it, mostly in the tropics, and most of those in Africa. If malaria could be eliminated, much human suffering conceivably could be relieved. This chapter will consider this possibility. It is important to remember that the future is always uncertain.

THE ROLE OF GENES

In 1990, the United States began its part in the Human Genome Project, an international venture to determine the location of each gene on every human chromosome. Part of the goal of the project is to better understand diseases with genetic components and hopefully to eventually conquer them.

In the process, however, scientists have learned about the nature of genes in general and the biochemical processes that govern life. Moreover, they have gathered extensive knowledge about the genes and heredity of other forms of life as well because the technology that was learned in mapping the human genome was applied to other forms of life.

If, or perhaps more appropriately when, the genome of the malaria protozoa can be determined, the development of a vaccine against them will be much more likely, as described below.

THE IMMUNE SYSTEM

Some of the proteins that are produced by cells result from the unique combination of genes that an individual inherits. Of those unique proteins, some end up on cell surfaces, where they biochemically identify the individual who carries them. They essentially identify him or her as "self." Thus, when a disease organism with its unique genes and unique cell surface proteins enters a human body, it is recognized as "non-self."

The identification proteins of a parasite are recognized as foreign or **antigens** (Figure 9.1). The host responds by trying to reject the parasites. The host can reject the antigens by producing **antibodies** (Figure 9.2), chemicals that attempt to destroy the invader's antigens produced by one set of white blood cells called **lymphocytes** or by directly attacking the antigen with another set of lymphocytes.

The mechanism by which the body fights an infection is quite similar to the mechanism by which it tries to reject a transplanted organ. For example, a transplanted heart has the identification proteins of the donor individual. In an organ recipient, those proteins would be considered antigens and would trigger an **immune response**. This process is called tissue rejection. When someone develops an infection, the immune system recognizes the antigens and attempts to reject them. When somebody receives a donated organ, he or she is given immunosuppressant drugs to prevent organ rejection. The organ recipient must be kept in an environment that is nearly sterile because of great risk of infection from suppression of the immune system.

In a healthy person, the biochemical monitors that respond to antigens would typically respond to disease organisms. In

THE FUNCTIONING OF GENES

Genes are units of chemical information that are found inside cells. They are responsible for every trait that an organism shows. Genes are located on chromosomes, which are long strands of deoxyribonucleic acid (DNA) found in the nuclei of cells. Each gene is a unit of that DNA that codes for or dictates the production of a specific protein. That gene first makes a modified copy of itself called messenger RNA, which then travels from the nucleus into the cell's cytoplasm. There, a ribosome assembles the protein out of amino acids. Whenever DNA spontaneously changes, or mutates, the result is ultimately a change in the protein that is produced.

Proteins play a number of very important roles in the life of a cell. Some are responsible for how a cell, and therefore an organism, is put together. Others are chemical regulators, called enzymes, that control chemical reactions. In multicellular animals like ourselves, some proteins are produced in response to infection. Such proteins are known as *antibodies*. They function specifically in response to disease organisms or, in some cases, to chemical products of disease organisms, such as waste products.

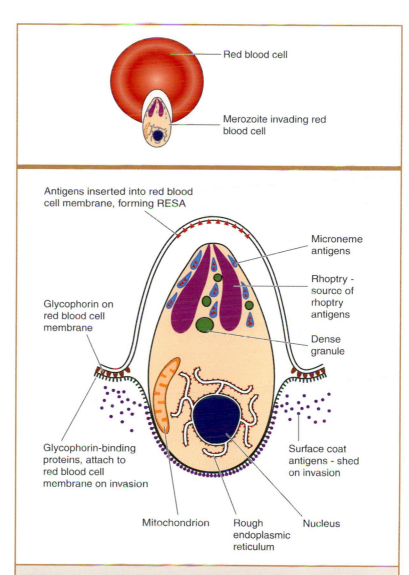

Figure 9.1 *Plasmodia* antigens are very complex, as can be seen in this figure. Antigens form on both the surface of the cell (such as antigens inserted into the cell membrane, top, and surface coat antigens). Other antigens form within the cell itself (microneme antigens). All types of antigens alert the immune system to the presence of a foreign object. The immune system then sends out antigens that attempt to destroy the invading cell.

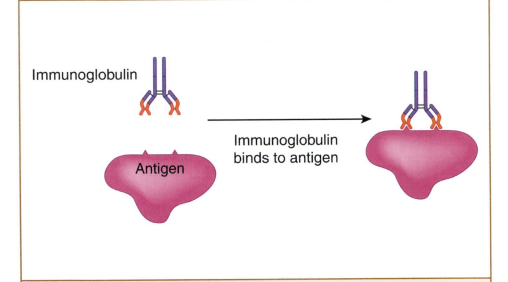

Figure 9.2 The human body creates antibodies in response to foreign antigens. These antibodies, shaped like a "Y," attach to the foreign body at the antigen-presenting site and eventually destroy the invading organism before it can cause harm to the body.

nature, the response to a disease organism, the immune response, offers long term, sometimes permanent, protection if it is successful. To bring about immune protection medically without inducing illness, doctors use **vaccines**.

In the case of malaria, the parasites involved in the initial attack are few in number. They circulate in the bloodstream for a very short time. Therefore, the immune system does not get much chance to detect them. Consequently, for a malarial vaccine to work, it would not only have to be administered before infection occurred, it would also have to be sufficiently modified to remain in circulation for enough time for the immune system to react.

Most successful vaccines have been developed to combat viral diseases, such as polio or smallpox. Some have been developed against bacterial diseases as well, but not as many. Viruses are genetically simple organisms. Bacteria, although more complex than viruses, are still relatively uncomplicated organisms.

Malaria is caused by protozoans, which are eukaryotic cells and, therefore, more genetically and biochemically complex. That genetic complexity allows *Plasmodium*, the malaria protozoan, to adapt quickly to changes in its environment, which is what a new medication would amount to. Consequently, malaria can and does develop resistance to drugs rapidly. The genetic complexity also allows the parasite

DISEASE PREVENTION BY VACCINATION

When a person develops an infectious disease, his or her body responds by producing proteins called antibodies, which protect the body. The antibodies are produced in response to antigens, proteins on the surface of the infecting organism. They may dissolve the antigens, they may cause them to clump together, or they may simply bind them up so that they can do no harm. This response is called an immune response. If the response is quick and strong enough, the person will recover from the infection. If not, he or she may die. When and if recovery occurs, the antibodies will remain protective, in some cases for life. This period of protection is immunity.

Immunities can be medically induced. If an antigen is medically introduced into a person, by a vaccine, the recipient will respond by developing antibodies, just as if he or she had the disease. A vaccine contains the antigens that will stimulate the production of antibodies.

Usually, the antigens that are introduced are not unadulterated disease germs. They have been weakened or killed. As long as intact antigens are present, however, our bodies cannot tell whether they are dangerous or not, and our immune system responds as if the antigen presents a real threat.

to change antigens quickly, which helps it hide from the immune system. This ability to change makes the task of developing a vaccine extremely difficult because a vaccine that works against one set of malarial antigens will not work against altered ones.

Coincidentally, the virus that causes influenza ("the flu") is genetically more complex than most viruses, changes antigens frequently, and keeps evolving resistance to vaccines. That is why new flu vaccines are needed every year. Because malaria is even more complex than the flu, developing effective vaccines would be much more difficult.

Certain political realities stand in the way of developing a vaccine. Because malaria is most common in some of the poorest countries in the world, there is not a lot of research money to support the search for new drugs or vaccines, nor are there research facilities in which to do the work. Even Roll Back Malaria, an internationally funded program, can function only as long as the foundations and their sponsors are willing to continue providing funds. Roll Back Malaria is, however, researching a vaccine. Research on a malaria vaccine is also being conducted in Australia. Malaria does not have the visibility of another plague that is also rampant in Africa with which it coexists and competes for research money: AIDS.

Unlike malaria, AIDS has a very real presence in the United States. Although AIDS is not the biggest killer in North America, it reportedly garners the most research money largely because it is so visible. AIDS has affected celebrities. It has received attention from a lot of celebrities and politicians. In contrast, malaria is well hidden. It does not have a cast of celebrities to advertise its existence. It does not occur, at the moment, in the United States. However, it continues to fester in Africa and Asia, and it continues to take lives daily. Continued support for malaria research is as important as is support for AIDS research.

WHAT WILL THE FUTURE BRING WITH MALARIA?

Once again, the future is uncertain. There is no way of knowing, for example, if malaria will ever return to the United States in epidemic proportions. The reality is that it could. The scenarios by which it could happen were described in Chapter 8.

It is also possible that the research on malaria may lead to the successful development of a vaccine. However, this development will require much more research and information.

In addition to poverty and remoteness of the lands where it is now rampant, there are other obstacles to conquering malaria. In those places, population growth is very rapid, there is a lot of crowding, and sick people are sometimes lost within the masses. There is political instability in some of those places, and some are socially unstable as well. There is hunger as well as illness, and often there is no easy way of getting food and medicines to the people who need them.

Technically speaking, developing a vaccine for malaria is probably well within the realm of possibility. But malaria is only one of many things that is competing for the attention of the limited scientific, medical, and humanitarian resources that are available. One would hope that the problems with malaria, as well as all of the other problems facing the world today, will one day be solved. At this point, however, that remains to be seen.

Diseases such as mumps and rubella have been brought under control as a result of vaccination. Smallpox was eliminated from nature using vaccines. Some cultures of smallpox virus have been artificially maintained, some of them for the purpose of biological warfare. Not all disease organisms lend themselves to vaccine production, however. Vaccines seem to work best against viruses and, to a lesser extent, against bacteria. Parasitic protozoa and more complex parasites such as worms seem to be better able to hide from

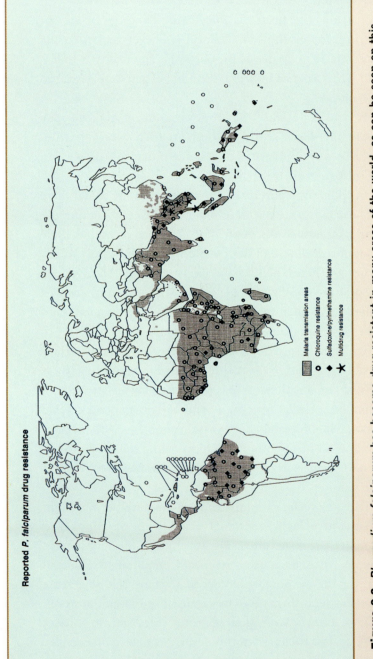

Figure 9.3 *Plasmodium falciparum* has become drug resistant in many areas of the world, as can be seen on this map. Areas designated by a circle contain *Plasmodium* that are resistant to chloroquine. Areas marked with a star contain organisms that are resistant to many different drugs, including chloroquine.

the immune system. Consequently, vaccines against them are much more challenging to produce.

Malaria has been a dangerous companion of the human race for as long as the human race has existed and perhaps even longer. Fifty years ago, it seemed as if malaria would be eliminated. Today, malaria is once again rampant in much of the world, killing hundreds of thousands and making millions ill. Moreover, today many strains of malaria are resistant to many of the medications that have worked against them in the past. The mosquito vectors that spread the disease have developed resistance to many pesticides and drugs (Figure 9.3). Malaria stands ready to threaten much of the rest of the world as well. Research goes on to conquer malaria, by vaccine and by medication. Research is also in progress to develop new, safe, and effective treatments.

Glossary

Alternation of Generations — A life cycle characterized by alternating sexually and asexually reproducing generations.

Alternative Host — A host, other than a parasite's usual host, in which a parasite can survive and complete its life cycle.

Antibiotic — A chemical usually produced by a microorganism that has the capacity to kill or otherwise inhibit other microorganisms but are usually not sufficiently toxic to humans or other animals to prevent their use medically.

Antibody — A blood protein that is produced in response to an infection and is toxic or otherwise inhibitory to the infecting organism.

Antigen — A chemical, usually on the surface of a cell, that can stimulate the production of antibodies in an organism.

Arthropod — An animal characterized by having a hard, jointed body covering, no internal skeleton, and paired, jointed legs.

Bioaccumulation — The buildup of environmental toxins or contaminants in predatory animals or other higher-level consumers.

Bioterrorism — Using biological agents such as disease germs or toxins in an act of war or in act of intimidating a population.

Bioweapon — A biological agent, usually of a pathogenic nature, used to deliberately harm others.

DDT — Dichloro-diphenyl-trichloroethane, an insecticide used to kill mosquitoes.

Definitive Host — The host in which a parasite usually reaches sexual maturity.

Diploid — The normal chromosome number in cells other than reproductive cells. It is characterized by chromosomes capable of being arranged in pairs, with one member of each pair having been donated by one of two parents. In humans, the diploid chromosome number is 46.

Ecotourism — Tourism with the specific intent of visiting unique environments.

Ectoparasite — An organism that lives on the surface of a host organism, obtains nourishment from the host, and can potentially cause harm.

Endoparasite — An organism that lives within a host organism, obtains nourishment from the host, and can potentially cause harm.

Haploid — The number of chromosomes normally found in a reproductive cell. It is equal to half of the diploid number, which in humans amounts to 23.

Host—An organism on or in which a parasite lives.

Immune Response—The reaction of an organism to infection, often characterized by fever and the increased production of white blood cells.

Immunity—Resistance to infection, often due to the presence of circulating antibodies in the blood stream.

Insecticide—A chemical used specifically to kill insects.

Intermediate Host—An organism in which a parasite must spend most of its life cycle but in which it does not reach sexual maturity.

Lymphocyte—A white blood cell that participates in long-term immune responses, either by producing circulating antibodies or by producing cells that directly attack an antigen.

Meiosis—The form of cell division in which chromosome number is cut by half, that is in which haploid cells are produced. This usually occurs in the production of reproductive cells.

Parasite—An organism that lives on or in a host organism, obtains its nourishment from the host, and has the potential of causing harm.

Pathogen—A parasite that specifically causes disease.

Pesticide—A chemical that is used to kill or inhibit pest organisms.

Reservoir Host—The organism in which a parasite is normally found in nature.

Vaccine—A chemical made from weakened or otherwise nonpathogenic antigens from infectious organisms that is medically administered to a person or animal in order to generate an immunity.

Vector—Usually, but not always, an ectoparasite that can transmit disease organisms among hosts.

Zoonosis—A disease of animals that can be transmitted to and infect people.

Bibliography

Anderson, K.E. *Malaria, Mosquitoes and Mayhem*. Bethel, Conn.: Carlton Press Co., 1988.

Aslan, G., M. Ulukanligil, A. Seyrek, and O. Erel. "Diagnostic Performance Characteristics of Rapid Dipstick Test for *Plasmodium vivax* Malaria." *Membrias do Instituto Oswaldo Cruz On-line*, Vol. 95, No. 5, pp. 683-686, 2001. Available at *http://memorias.loc.fiocruz.br/965/4147.pdf*

Attaran, A., R. Maharaj, and R. Lirof. "Ethical Debate: Doctoring Malaria Badly: The Global Campaign to Ban DDT." *British Medical Journal*, Vol. 321, 2000, pp. 1403-1405.

Baldwin, C. *Sickle Cell Disease*. Chicago: Heinemann Library, 2003.

Ballard, C. *The Immune System*. Chicago: Heinemann Library, 2003.

Bannister, L.H., J.M. Hopkins, R.E. Fowler, S. Krishna, and G.H. Mitchell. "Encyclopedia of Malaria: Asexual Blood Stage." *Parasitology Today*, Vol. 16, 2000, pp. 427-433.

Becker, N. *Mosquitoes and their Control*. New York: Kluwer Academic/Plenem Publishers, 2003.

Borza, N. "Some Observations on Malaria and the Ecology of Central Macedonia in Antiquity." *American Journal of Ancient History* Vol. 4, No. 1, 1979, pp. 102-124.

Bwire, R. *Bugs in Armor: a Tale of Malaria and Soldiering*. Lincoln, Nebr.: IUniverse, Inc., 2000.

Carson, R.L. *Silent Spring*. New York: Houghton Mifflin Co., 1962.

Cartwright, F.F. and M. Biddis. *Disease and History*, 2nd Ed., Phoenix Mill, U.K.: Sutton Publishing Ltd., 2000.

Casman, E.A. and H. Dowlatabadi (Eds.) *The Contextual Determinants of Malaria*. Washington, D.C., Resources for the Future, 2002.

Chernin, J. *Parasitology*. New York: Taylor and Francis, Inc., 2000.

Clements, A.N. *The Biology of Mosquitoes: Vol. 2: Sensory Reception and Behaviour*. New York: Oxford University Press. 1999.

Crepley, I.M., D.N.J. Lockwood, D. Mack, G. Pasvol, and R.N. Davidson. "Rapid Diagnosis of Falciparum Malaria by using ParaSight F Test in Travellers Returning to the United Kingdom: Prospective Study." *British Medical Journal*, Vol. 321, 2002, pp. 484-485.

Commoner, B. *The Closing Circle*. New York: Bantam Books, 1972.

Davis, K. *Cracking the Genome: Inside the Race to Unlock Human DNA*. Baltimore: Johns Hopkins University Press, 2002.

Day, N. *Malaria, West Nile, and other Mosquito-Borne Diseases*. Berkely Heights, N.J.: Enslow Publishers, Inc., 2001.

Desalle, R. *Epidemic! The World of Infectious Disease.* New York: The New Press, 1999.

Diamond, J. *Guns, Germs, and Steel: the Fates of Human Societies.* New York: W.W. Norton & Company, 1997.

Donaldson, R.J. (Ed.). *Parasites and Western Man.* Baltimore: University Park Press, 1979.

Doolan, D.L. (Ed.). *Malaria: Methods and Protocols.* Totowa, N.J.: Humana Press, 2003.

DuTemple, L.A. *The Panama Canal.* Minneapolis: Lerner Publishing Group, 2002.

Ewald, P.W. *Evolution of Infectious Disease.* New York: Oxford University Press, 1994.

Fradin, M.S. "Mosquitoes and Mosquito Repellents: A Clinician's Guide." *Annals of Internal Medicine,* Vol. 128, June, 1998, pp. 931-940.

Freudenrich, C.C. "How Mosquitoes Work." *How Stuff Works,* 2000. Available at *http://www.howstuffworks.com*

Harrison, G. *Malaria, Mosquitoes, and Man: A History of Hostilities Since 1880.* New York: Dutton, 1978.

Hausmann, K. and N. Hülsmann. *Protozoology.* New York: Thieme Medical Publishers, Inc., 1996.

Honigsbaum, M. *The Fever Trail: In Search of the Cure for Malaria.* New York: Picador, 2003.

Jarcho, S. *Quinine's Predecessor: Francisco Torti and the Early History of Cinchona.* Baltimore: John's Hopkins University Press, 1993.

Karlen, A. *Men and Microbes: Disease and Plagues in History and Modern Times.* New York: Simon & Schuster, 1996.

"Malaria, Mosquitoes, and DDT." *World Watch,* Vol. 15, Issue 3, May/June 2002.

Matteson, P. *Resolving the DDT Dilemma: Protecting Biodiversity and Human Health.* Collingdale, Pa.: Diane Publishing Co., 2002.

McNeill, W.H. *Plagues and People.* Harden City, N.Y.: Anchor Press, 1976.

Mohr, N. *Malaria: Evolution of a Killer.* Seattle, Wash.: Serif & Pixel Press, 2001.

Morrison, P. and P. Morrison. "Roll Back Malaria." *Scientific American,* January, 2000.

Oldstone, M.B. *Viruses, Plagues, and History.* New York: Oxford University Press, 2000

Bibliography

Pampana, E. *Textbook of Malaria Eradication.* New York: Oxford University Press, 1970.

Poser, C.M. and G.W. Bruyn. *An Illustrated History of Malaria.* New York: The Parthenon Publishing Group, 1999.

Reid, A.J.C., C.S.M. Whitty, H.M. Ayles, R.M. Jennings, B.A. Bovill, J.M. Felton, R.H. Behrens, A.D.M. Bryceson, and D.C.W. Mabey. "Malaria at Christmas: Risks of Prophylaxis versus Risks of Malaria." *British Medical Journal*, 317, 1998, pp. 1506-1508.

Schmidt, G.D., L.S. Roberts, and J. Janovy Jr. *Foundations of Parasitology.* New York: McGraw-Hill Science/Engineering/Math, 1995.

Scientific American. "A Death Every 30 Seconds." June, 2002. Available at *http://www.sciam.com*

"Scientist Discovers Mosquito Repellent in Tomatoes." *Science News,* June 11, 2002. Available at *http://www.cosmiverse.com/news/science/science06110103.html*

Sellares, R. *Malaria and Rome: A History of Malaria in Ancient Italy.* New York: Oxford University Press, 2002.

Shulka, O.P. *Pesticides, Man and Biosphere.* New Delhi, India: Ashish Publishing House, 1998.

Spielman, A. and M. D'Antonio. *Mosquito: A Natural History of our most Persistent and Deadly Foe.* New York: Hyperion, 2001.

Sugden, A.L. and J. Chamberlain (Eds.) *Malaria: Current Topics & Reviews.* Champaign, Ill.: Pharmaceutical Press, 1997.

Sutherland, D.J. and W.J. Crans. *Mosquitoes in Your Life.* New Jersey Agriculture Experiment Station Publication SA220-5M-86, 1986. Available at *http://www-rci.Rutgers.edu/~insects/moslife.htm.*

Sweeny, A.W. "Prospects for Control of Mosquito-Borne Diseases." *Journal of Medical Microbiology,* Vol. 48, No. 10, 1999, pp. 879-881.

Textbook of Malaria Eradication. New York: Oxford University Press, 1970.

Travis, J. "Blood Cues Sex Choices for Parasite." *Science News Online, January 8.* Available at *http://www.findarticles.com/cf_dis/m1200/2_157/58726365/p1/article*

Tren, R., R. Bate, and H.M. Koenig. *Malaria and the DDT Story.* London: Institute of Economic Affairs, 2001.

Turkington, C.A. *Ills and Conditions: Malaria.* 1999. Available at *http://www.principalhealthnews.com/topic/malaria.*

Walker, H. "We Remember . . . The Erie Canal," Newark, N.Y.: *The Newark Courier Gazette*, March 18, 1998. Available at *http://cgazette.com/towns/Newark/history/918323473038.htm*

Warrell, D.A. and H.M. Gilles. *Essential Malariology*, 4th Ed. London: Edward Arnold Publisher, 2002.

Watts, S. *Epidemics and History: Disease, Power, and Imperialism.* New Haven, Conn.: Yale University Press, 1997.

Williams, G. *The Plague Killers.* New York: Charles Scribner's & Sons. 1969.

Wong, K. Combating Malaria. *Scientific American.* October, 2000. Available at *http://www.sciam.com*

— "Research Challenges Proposed Link Between Malaria Growth and Global Warming." *Scientific American.* February, 2002. Available at *http://www.sciam.com*

World Health Organization. *DDT and its Derivatives: Environmental Aspects.* Albany, N.Y.: World Health Organization Publishing, 1989.

World Health Organization. *Vector Control for Malaria and other Mosquito-Borne Diseases: Report of a WHO Study Group.* Albany, N.Y.: WHO Publication Ctr., 1995.

World Watch Institute. *State of the World: 2003.* New York: W.W. Norton & Co., 2002.

Zookerman, J.N. *Essentials of Travel Medicine.* Hoboken, N.J.: John Wiley & Sons, 2003.

Websites

The American Mosquito Control Association
http://www.mosquito.org/mosquito.html

Biology at Marietta College
Information about Bioaccumulation
http://www.marietta.edu/~biol/102/2bioma95.html

Centers for Disease Control and Prevention
http://www.cdc.gov

Extoxnet
Information about Pesticides
http://ace.orst.edu/info/extoxnet/pips/deltamet.htm

Malaria Foundation International
http://www.malaria.org

Malaria Online Research Source, History of Malaria
http://www.rph.wa.gov.au/labs/haem/malaria/history.html

Malaria Site
http://www.malariasite.com/

Malaria Vaccine
European Malaria Vaccine Consortium
http://www.euromalvac.org/

Malaria Vaccine Initiative
http://www.malariavaccine.org/files/0301-newleadership.htm

Medical Ecology of Malaria
http://www.medicalecology.org/disease/malaria/d_malaria.html#sect4

MedicineNet.com
http://www.medicinenet.com/malaria/page1.htm

Medilinks
http://www.medilinks.org/HealthTopics/Communicable_Diseases/Malaria/
    Malaria.htm

Mosquito Buzz
Information about Mosquitoes and Prevention
http://www.mosquitobuzz.com/

National Cancer Institute, Understanding the Immune System
http://press2.nci.nih.gov/sciencebehind/immune/immune01.htm

National Geographic's Website about Parasites
http://www.nationalgeographic.com/parasites/splashframe.html

National Library of Medicine
http://www.nlm.nih.gov

New Jersey Agriculture Experiment Station
Information about Mosquitoes and their Lifestyle
http://www.rci.rutgers.edu/~insects/moslife.htm

Parasitology Image List
Micrographs of various parasites, including *Plasmodium*
http://www.life.sci.qut.edu.au/LIFESCI/darben/protozoa.htm

Parasitology Online
http://www.parasitology-online.com

Roll Back Malaria
http://www.rbm.who.int

Sickle Cell Disease Association of America, Inc.
http://sicklecelldisease.org

Smithsonian Institution Libraries Information on Malaria
http://www.sil.si.edu/Exhibitions/Make-the-Dirt-Fly/bugwar.html

U.S. Environmental Protection Agency
http://www.epa.gov

The Walter and Eliza Hall Institute Malaria Database, part of the
    University of Leicester
http://www.wehi.edu.au/MalDB-www/intro.html

The Wellcome Trust
Information about Malaria and *Plasmodium*
http://www.wellcome.ac.uk

World Health Organization
http://www.who.int

World Health Organization/Tropical Disease Research Information
http://www.wehi.edu.au/MalDB-www/who.html

Index

Index

Picture Credits

9: Data from Statistical Health Reports, Division of Medical Statistics, Office of the Surgeon General, Department of the Army
12: © Richard Walters/Visuals Unlimited
18: Lambda Science Artwork
23: © Biodisc/Visuals Unlimited
24: © WHO/PIERRE VIROT
28: Lambda Science Artwork
29: © Biodisc/Visuals Unlimited
30: Courtesy Agricultural Research Service (ARS), US Department of Agriculture
36: © Biodisc/Visuals Unlimited
44: © The Nobel Foundation
47: © Gianni Dagli Ori/CORBIS
51: © Noelle Nardone

55: Photo by Scott Bauer, Courtesy ARS, US Department of Agriculture
61: © Noelle Nardone
62: Courtesy CDC, Public Image Health Library
65: © Galen Rowell/CORBIS
70: © WHO/PIERRE VIROT
71: © WHO/PIERRE VIROT
77: Courtesy World Health Organization, Roll Back Malaria
78: Data from World Health Report 2001, WHO
85: Lambda Science Artwork
86: Lambda Science Artwork
90: WHO Technical Report Series, *WHO Expert Committee on Malaria*, 2000

Cover: © Lester V. Bergman/CORBIS

Off is a registered trademark of S.C. Johnson Company; Cutter is a registered trademark of Spectrum Brands; Malarone is a registered trademark of GlaxoSmithKline; Skin-So-Soft is a registered trademark of Avon Products, Inc.

About the Author

Bernard A. Marcus, Ph.D. is professor of biology at Genesee Community College in Batavia, New York. His principal interests have been in environmental biology, particularly aquatics, and the modeling of aquatic environments in the laboratory. He has been involved in studies on New York's Finger Lakes, the impact of acid precipitation in the Adirondack Mountains, and the effects of water pollution on stream insects. More recently he has become interested in tropical biology and has been leading student trips to the rainforests of Central America. His recreational activities include fishing, hiking, and model railroading.

About the Editor

The late I. Edward Alcamo was a Distinguished Teaching Professor of Microbiology at the State University of New York at Farmingdale. Alcamo studied biology at Iona College in New York and earned his M.S. and Ph.D. degrees in microbiology at St. John's University, also in New York. He had taught at Farmingdale for over 30 years. In 2000, Alcamo won the Carski Award for Distinguished Teaching in Microbiology, the highest honor for microbiology teachers in the United States. He was a member of the American Society for Microbiology, the National Association of Biology Teachers, and the American Medical Writers Association. Alcamo authored numerous books on the subjects of microbiology, AIDS, and DNA technology as well as the award-winning textbook *Fundamentals of Microbiology*, now in its sixth edition.